THE LIGHT WITHIN

MY JOURNEY HOME
...TO...
THE WHITE BUFFALO

CYNTHIA HART-BUTTON, D.D.

SIRIUS.A PRESS
Sedona, Arizona

*I want to dedicate this book
to my Father, Mother, my sister Claudia
my children & my three nieces*

SIRIUS.A PRESS
Attn: SWPA
80 Juniper Drive
Sedona, Arizona 86336

Copyright 2018 by Cynthia Hart-Button

All rights reserved. No part of this book may be reproduced or utilized in any form or by any means, electronic or mechanical, including photocopying, recording, or by any information storage and retrieval system, without permission in writing from the publisher.

ISBN 9781984056429 (paperback) ISBN 1984056425 (e-book)

Printed and bound in the United States by Amazon Publishing, Inc. A percentage of the sale of this book goes to support the White Bison Herd.

To send correspondence to the author of this book, mail a first-class letter to the author at: Cynthia Hart-Button, 12635 Wyatt Run Road, Amesville OH 45711 or contact the author directly at www.cynthiahart.com, www.whitebisonassociation.com by email at mystichart@msn.com or phone at (805)400-7866.

Contents

Foreword by Linda Tucker   14
Introduction/Flashback   16

Chapter 1   My Father's Death   22
Chapter 2   The Journey Begins   31
Chapter 3   The Fire Walk   34
Chapter 4   Meeting at the Coffee Pot   38
Chapter 5   The Search   45
Chapter 6   The Prayer Pipe   51
Chapter 7   Coincidence   58
Chapter 8   The Cascade Mountains   61
Chapter 9   Firewood   64
Chapter 10   Confronting Fear   68
Chapter 11   The Lodge   72
Chapter 12   The Medicine Wheel   79
Chapter 13   Preparing for Winter   88
Chapter 14   Viewing other Worlds   96
Chapter 15   Rabbit Stew   103
Chapter 16   The Mushroom Journey   107
Chapter 17   My Wolf Bear Bear   113
Chapter 18   The End of My Year   121
Chapter 19   My Vision from Sundance   125

Postscript   132

Acknowledgments

When my father died in 1988, I was very lost and confused. He was always my pillar of strength and security. Some days he took me on horseback up the hill to pray to Creator. He always told me, "Never go back to your past. If it was important, it would still be there." "Don't judge people. If you do, you are judging yourself." "See people as a mirror in your life and always try to figure out why they are there." "Remember, you don't have to engage in everybody's drama. You can just be a spectator and walk away." "Most of all, love yourself for who you are. Don't ever worry what people think or say about you. Stand in your own conviction and people will see who you truly are."

Along my path, over the last 30 years since then, I met very important teachers and dear friends who have guided me. All of those who helped, became the mirrors that inspired me to learn a certain key aspect of healing.

The first of these are my late Mom, Phyllis Guss, my grandmother Edith Kom, my sister Claudia and my eldest daughter Renee. I want to thank my other two daughters, who chose to live with their father during the crucial last years of his life and were too young at the time to understand what I was going through. They fulfilled an important role for our family with this good man. I am proud and love them both as successful mothers and career women. My Mom taught me about the Welsh spiritual heritage of our family. Descended from a long line of psychics, Mom enrolled me at Lily Dale where I studied with key teachers of intuitive sciences in New York. My grandmother Edith Kom was also an inspiration whose book of herbal remedies I found very useful. My sister Claudia has always been my highest encouragement because she always believed in what I do. We have a unique sisterhood. I am so proud to call her my sister and I love her very much. My dear daughter Renee traveled with me as I took my first unsteady steps on my Path. We have always been honest with each other, through thick and thin and she always wanted to be at my side no matter how intense it was. You are my daughter, a great mother and career woman, wise beyond your years. We grew up together, I love you and I think of you more as a true sister than anything else.

"Lucky", White Wind, an Ohio Cherokee medicine man, my Dad's best friend, was there for me before during and in the crucial time after my father's death. He helped me to find my path and open the medicine ways of my Native American side. White Wind gave me my first Cherokee prayer pipe which marked a very important time in my connection to Creator. The pipe my Dad wanted me to return to the Nation began my quest to Spirit and Lucky's gift pipe began my understanding of how to pray. I buried my father's personal pipe after I received my own personal white buffalo calf pipe from Lone Wolf. It has been blessed by many elders.

I want to thank the dear Ohio and Michigan friends and colleagues of my 20s, Elizabeth Howell and Sandy Raines, who continue on the path to Spirit beside me today. I also want to acknowledge Sandy's late mother, my teacher, Tommy Raines. Also in the 80s, I thank my dear friend Carol Shaheen for giving me my first computer and introducing me to many great friends. I also want to thank my colleagues at the Michigan Unity Church.

I want to thank the masterful and well-known teachers that I met in my 20 years in Sedona, Colorado and Hawaii. Dr. Houston, my teacher of contact healing in Sedona, Hannah Kroger my teacher of herbal medicine in Boulder. My dear friend and teacher of spiritual nutrition, Rabbi Gabriel Cousens, M.D. and his wife Shanti Golds-Cousens have been constant friends and advisors. A special thank you to Linda Tucker, Guardian of the White Lions for her support of me and the White Buffalo on this journey. I want to thank 21st Century Radio Host, Zohara Hieronimus for her book *White Spirit Animals: Prophets of Change* which includes my work with the White Buffalo among profiles of other white animal caretakers. I want to thank Paul Hait, Phil Cook and Pendleton Woolen Mills for making the Chief Hiawatha, Big Medicine Blanket the symbol for the Herd.

Harriet McMahon, "Red Hawk" my colleague at the summer Spirit Quest gatherings has brought the sacred Andean shamanic traditions to our students and a great deal of love and support. Jean Gita Fisher, "Black Buffalo Woman," tended the Lodge and fires and always showed-up to bring grace and healings to our gatherings and our personal health. Our dear departed sister, Rain On The Earth was a dear friend and great supporter of the Herd. Joseph Seidell and his family have been a constant source of love and support since the moment we met and I adopted him as a son.

My great Native teacher-friends I'd like to thank and honor are many from all over the U.S.: "Lucky," White Wind for fulfilling my Dad's dream and putting me back on the Path, Leonard Crow Dog, Hollis Littlecreek, Red Ute, Wallace Black Elk, Will Sampson, Lone Wolf, Jayne and Anita Polacca, my adopted Hopi parents, White Bear, Shane and Michael Big Bear. My true inspirations are Black Elk, who dictated his important memoire *Black Elk Speaks* to John Neihardt and my great ancestor, Sitting Bull.

From my years in Sedona, I want to thank my dear friends Bishop Larry Jensen and Bishop Glenda Green, founders of Spiritis Church, Marylou Keller of the Unity Church of Sedona, the late Robert Archer and Kristen Monday, my roommate Johnny Appleseed, my friend Raymond and my friends at the Medicine Wheels at Schnebly Hill. I want to give special thanks to my spirit animals Wolfa, Bear Bear, Buddy and Buddha, Boo and Blackie, the wolves that have walked with me on my life's Journey. My dear departed cat Mau, an Egyptian Mau cat, hiked and walked everywhere with me. You are dearly missed all of you. And to the White Buffalos for all of your great teachings and for accepting me into your family as part of the Herd. It has been a great challenge and always an incredible experience.

I want to thank three very special people who have done so much to bring the White Buffalo home. Melanie Sweet, you have helped me think outside the box of what conservation can look like in 101 ways. You've given me the gift of hope when I was sure there was none. Pat Elton you are such a dear friend and advisor on land use issues and so much more. With you here, I know we will always "get it right." And to our very generous and visionary unnamed Ambassador: without you this Herd would still be on the roam. You have given us the thing we needed most, a big, beautiful Ohio farm and ranch with plentiful land and water where the Herd will not only live but thrive.

What inspired me to write the book were authors that came to Sedona to talk about their books on spirituality. A key person I met at the book talks who encouraged me to write my own story was astrologer Cheryl Rose. She listened and told me I needed to write and publish my story. My great friend and digital medical records entrepreneur Marilyn Gard, lent her organizational skill to put my thoughts into order for the layman reader. Years later, my husband Charles Button and his sister Sandy Fields provided painstaking editorial expertise on the manuscript. Charles came into my life at the beginning of the Journey of the White Buffalo, stood next to me as a great partner and has also devoted his life to the Herd. With constant and loving support, Charles, you have always had my back and my heart. My dear friend, evolutionary astrologer, Kari Noren-Hoshal became the final editor to get the book to digital format and print. Kari has been one of my greatest friends and supporters on my Journey. Our husbands have patiently put up with our Sirius shenanigans as "twin sisters." Thank you for being in my life.

Foreword

Cynthia's life-story is an inspirational real-life legend told by an extraordinary woman of great courage, perseverance and, most of all, heart-connection with Mother Earth. A woman who has survived in a frozen cave with a pack of wolves, raised their young, and heard their wisdom. A woman who has fought human prejudice and brutality, to speak for the animals. A woman who is fighting still to protect a herd of White Bison against seemingly impossible odds. A story of a woman in crisis, torn between the dictates of a modern world bent on destruction and her deepest ancestral roots which chart the path to redemption.

Unusual as the circumstances may be, there are secrets revealed here that we should all hear which light the way to restoring hope in our lives and preserving life of this planet. The White Bison, like the rare White Lions, whom I am honored to protect, in the heart of their natural kingdom, are Sacred Messengers. They are Nature's greatest blessing but also her final warning. How can they be both a blessing and a warning?

In an ideal world, the great White Bison would be roaming the wilderness plains along with the other creatures of their ecosystem, flourishing in freedom and sovereignty. They would be honored as a sacred gift from Mother Nature, loved and respected together with all natural creation. The fact that they have been held in camps for their own safety, by this intrepid woman who has dedicated her life and her resources to their safe-keeping, is a critically serious barometer of the fragility of our world. A man-made world, in which the wonders of Nature are no longer stewarded as a sacred heritage.

Instead, planetary mismanagement has brought us to the brink of collapse, where every species is fast becoming an endangered species, including our own. The return of the White Bison was prophesied by the sacred traditions of Native America from which Cynthia originates. Lakota Chief Arvol Looking Horse, 19th Generation Carrier of the White Buffalo Calf Pipe, shares their critical message for Peace and has stood immovable, like Standing Rock itself, for the sanctity of Nature.

Like the legendary White Lions which have suddenly appeared in the sacred site of Timba-vati in Africa, these sacred animals are directly linked to sacred sites. Their sudden arrival in our times offers hope, but equally demands that we face up to the urgency of changing our ways, before it is too late. This is the story of a woman who is attempting that. Gripping, daunting, quirky, uncompromising, Cynthia's journey home to the wisdom of the White Buffalo encourages each of us to unite in standing up for the protection of our beloved planet.

Linda Tucker
Guardian of the White Lions
Founder & CEO, Global White Lions Protection Trust
& The Linda Tucker Foundation

Introduction

When people ask about my childhood, I never know quite how to respond. I grew up with two parents, which unfortunately, is not the case for a lot of children these days. My father was Lakota, my mother a second-generation Welsh immigrant. My father's western name was Uriah Guss. His tribal name was White Buffalo. My father was the son of Arvo Guss, a Lakota born in South Dakota, and married to a woman of Irish heritage. Buffalo Bill Cody, of the well know Wild West Show, was a cousin to my grandfather by marriage. Buffalo Bill's actual last name was Guss, which I learned means "goose" in German.

Growing up I was told by family elders that when my grandfather was young, he was removed from his family, along with other Lakota boys his age. He was relocated to a school in Pennsylvania. From what I understand, Grandfather Arvo was taken away from his family and converted to Christianity. His Native American clothing and personal possessions were taken away from him and he was dressed in western clothing. His long hair was cut off and he was taught to read, write and speak English.

My grandfather became a rancher in the Harrisburg, Pennsylvania area where I was born. Buffalo Bill often came through town with his Wild West show and would stay with my grandparents. At the end of his life, Buffalo Bill became quite ill but continued to perform his shows. In gratitude for many years of their hospitality, Buffalo Bill gave my grandfather his famous silver saddle. He gave it to him at one of his last ever shows in Lewistown, PA. Within the year, he was dead.

The stories of Buffalo Bill's shows were often told by my grandfather to us kids when we were little. There was a tradition of showmanship in my family that we were familiar with and proud of. Spirituality however, was a different matter and much more confusing. My paternal grandmother came from a traditional Mennonite family. As he was growing up, my father's Sundays were spent at church and at big family suppers. My mother's Welsh background also made her a strong church goer. As adults, the men in our family seldom went to church except for one of my dad's brothers, Jerome.

Although my grandfather was converted to Christianity, I don't think he followed it much once he left the Carlisle School and began to work on his own ranch. My dad was much the same. If you asked him, my dad would say he believed in God and Christianity but would not go into a church. He believed that God was outside in nature. When I was little, Dad would get up on his horse and put me in front of him on the saddle. We would go up the hill and look out over the whole Tuscarora mountain range. My dad would never pray out loud. He would say a silent prayer and encourage me to do the same. "Just give thanks for everything around you," he said the first time. I replied, "I'd be up here all day if I had to give thanks for everything!" "That's the point, Dad said, "That's the point."

My one male church-going relative was my uncle, Jerome Guss. He was the preacher of the Gettysburg, PA Lutheran Church. Uncle Jerome had a fire and brimstone style of preaching. When I would go to church with my mother, he would rail and rant away at the people in the pews. To me, it sounded as if he was incredibly mad at them. I couldn't understand why he would be yelling at people who had come to listen to his teachings. One day I interrupted my preacher uncle mid-sermon to ask, "Uncle Jerome, why are you so mad? You should never fear God or Jesus, I said." Then I got up and walked out of the church. I got a good talking to over that one when I got home. The next time I saw Uncle Jerome, I told him that I would not come back to church if he was going to yell. "You're right little one, he said. You really are right."

While I was growing up on our homestead in the Tuscarora Mountains, my father built a number of businesses. He worked for Barnum and Bailey Circus as an animal handler and he had his own ranch, next to the one owned by my grandfather. My father was a tall, strong man with a gentle soul. He cared about people. He went out of his way to help them whenever possible. He was at home with nature and the great outdoors. He loved roses more than anything. He grew many prize-winning roses around our house. From him, I learned to study the earth cycles. And I learned about myself.

Because he could track people, my father was often called upon to find children lost in the state park down the road from our ranch. Late one afternoon a couple and another man appeared in our driveway. I was playing with my wolf in the grass nearby, and no one paid much attention to me, since I was only four years old. Suddenly, my wolf abruptly stopped playing and got in my face. I knew there was something going on that I should pay attention to. "Can you help us?" the man asked as he walked toward my father. "My son wandered off and we can't find him anywhere. My wife and I are frantic. He can't take care of himself and it's getting dark and cold out…"

My father was ready to help. "Give me a description," he said immediately."

"He's four years old," the man said. "He's got dark hair, brown eyes, and he's small for his age," the father's voice trailed off as he struggled for composure. He spoke as if hoping to awaken from a bad dream.

"What is he wearing? "Dad asked

"Let's ask my wife," the man said as he hurried toward his car. The adults didn't notice as I tagged along behind them.

"Honey, what was he wearing?" he asked.

"Blue jeans and a yellow tee shirt," the woman replied from the car. Having lived near the state park for years, my father knew the terrain. They would have to work fast to find the boy before nightfall. And they would have to be lucky.

I tugged at my father's arm. "I know where he is Dad," I said. "He's in a cave."

At first, my father seemed to ignore me. Then, he turned toward me curiously. He picked me up and set me on a fence post and asked, "How do you know that?"

"Because I can see him Dad. I see him in the cave. He's cold. He's scared. You have to get to him before the bears do." I implored my father. "I don't want him to get hurt."

My father stared straight into my eyes. Some fathers might have ignored the words of a child during such a stressful situation, but mine didn't. He knew I had been with him all day and wasn't just making something up. "Are you sure, Little Bear? "He said." Tell me what the cave looks like." My father knew I saw the world differently.

I told him about the landscape and location as I saw it. I described the cave walls and the smell of the grasses that partially covered the entrance. My father sent the couple back to their campsite in case their child had returned. He called for my wolf and gave the wolf the boy's scent by holding the child's blanket to its nose. Then we mounted one of our horses, with me in front. The man's friend walked and ran beside us as we made our way up through the tree line to the rocky caves at the base of the mountain.

We found the little boy before nightfall. I was four years old and my information had been correct. I had helped find my first missing person. As I look back now, I realize that I chose my parents wisely. Most adults would not have listened to the words of a child. My father honored me by hearing and believing in me. We all need to learn to honor ourselves. Sometimes I wonder if we know how.

Flashback

"Cynthia, you just got a fax. Do you want me to read it on the air?"
The disc jockey sat up in his chair, looking over the brief copy but made no attempt to hand it to me. I hesitated for only a second, mentally running through the possible senders of the fax. I didn't want something totally unexpected aired for a live radio audience, but I didn't pick up any psychic warnings, or cosmic red flags, as it were.

"Oh, sure why not read it?" I replied flippantly.

"To Cynthia Hart, Chief Button Pusher," he read with a hint of amusement. "Where's your book?"

I probably reacted with nervous laughter. A brief message, no sender's name, but I knew who had sent it.

"Do you think you could explain this somewhat bizarre nickname and the rest of the note?" To fill in time while I regained my composure, the D J repeated, "We have Cynthia Hart, nationally renowned psychic on the air with us this morning. She just received this fax at the station addressed to Chief Button Pusher and a cryptic message 'Where's your book?' Are you ready to explain, Cynthia?" His look was all innocence, as if he was honestly puzzled.

I explained "When I was in town last time, I gained the name Chief Button Pusher. Because I can see people's issues, I see them and I reflect them right back in their faces. I create chaos. I intentionally force people out of their comfort zones. When you push people's buttons, you make friends and enemies quick. The fax writer happens to be a friend of mine who thinks I deserve an amusing Indian name that describes my mission. Catchy, don't you think?"

The DJ responded "It's a great name. I can tell you from personal experience that it fits you perfectly. You've nailed a number of us here at the station on our issues. But, what about the second part -- where's your book? What does that mean?"

"You won't let me off the hook, will you?" I countered. Taking a deep breath, I decided to give the audience an honest, forthright answer instead of my usual avoidance. "This friend just pushed my biggest button. Spirit has been leading me toward writing a book, but my own issues keep getting in the way. Sometimes I don't feel worthy of being an author. I'm not sure I have anything to say that will help people. My button is self-worth and it's in my face again. I guess it's time to do something about it."

That interview was many years ago now. I wrote this manuscript over ten years ago and I've been preparing to publish this for quite a number of years. This is the first in a series of books about the White Buffalo and awakening to Spirit. It's about my spiritual journey. I don't believe my journey is any more important than anyone else's. It's more unusual perhaps, because of the ways in which Spirit has touched my life. But my hope is that something in this book will open your heart to Spirit and to examining your own connection with it.

I know there are a lot of people out there praying for me, for the White Buffalo and for this book. I thank you for your support. So, with love and light, my heart to your heart, let the journey begin....

1
My Father's Death

I was living in Bay Village, Ohio and working 60 hours a week for a 40-hour wage. Coming home from work one night a friend of mine said," Hey, let me give you a ride home. That car of yours is dangerous in the ice and snow."

Cleveland has some major winter storms. I was driving my little red Corvette and during my shift it had decided to snow, so I said yes and jumped in. On the way home, at 30th and Euclid, a drunken man ran the red light and hit us head on at 72 miles an hour.

I awoke to my mother's voice telling me "Come back. Your daughter needs you". I was about to face some pretty harsh music. I had taken a blow to the head. My skull was split and I had been in a coma for nine days. I was informed I had over one hundred broken bones. I would have to learn to walk, talk and remember things all over again. My identity was also shattered. I needed to find myself again.

My father came to me and said 'Think of the highest mountain in your mind and climb it to the top. Don't stop till you get there."

I took my Father's word literally. In my mind, the highest mountain in North America was Alaska's Mt. McKinley, so that's where I literally decided to move. I was involved with a Forestry Service survey on wolves in the Mt. McKinley area. I spent many long days freezing my legs off, waiting for wolves that I was watching to hunt on their territorial grounds. I've never been so cold in my life. I had to be out of my mind! I could have chosen the volcanos of Hawaii.

Let's jump ahead to a year and a half later. I was on Mt. McKinley, climbing with a Jr. Olympic team that happened to be training there that year. I wasn't

on the team. I was only helping out, but I was allowed to climb. We were having fun, but it was no picnic.
I learned there what the word "trudging" means. There comes a point where you can only move an arm or a leg, stop and wait. Then you gather up the will to move again.

We were high enough to need bottled oxygen. I remember I was just above a glacier with a baggy full of blue ice water I had just collected when I noticed my oxygen tank was running out.
I had been instructed to shoot the flare gun in an emergency or if I needed to be picked up. I was starting to become faint from lack of oxygen, so I set a flare off. It felt like I was falling asleep.

Suddenly, there was a man walking towards me accompanied by two strange looking goats. He looked like the Bonanza actor Lorne Greene and I thought I was hallucinating. Then, I noticed he was talking to me. I stammered, "What do you want?"

He promptly replied "I'm from Dog Star. I'm your Star Father and I have a serious mission. I want you to go back home to Ohio. You must warn the authorities of a possible nuclear power leak into the water of Lake Erie. There's going to be an earthquake. You have to warn them so they can move the dangerous material out."

I knew I was hallucinating but it was more than that. I thought I was going out of my mind. I looked down the mountain and to my surprise I saw this incredibly beautiful woman. She had long red hair and was standing with two strange-looking large goat-like creatures.

I remembered the Star Father's message but for some reason I was only half listening to this man. As he walked away I noticed that he didn't have any boots on. He was wearing a long beige and cobalt blue robe. He wore a beautiful piece of jewelry on his head. It was a gold symbol that looked like a greyhound.

Then I heard the helicopter. I forgot all about the dream until they had me loaded. I thought it was all my imagination. Abruptly turning to face me, the pilot in the helicopter said, "Who was that man you were talking to? What the hell was he doing there?" I was quiet the whole way back. I thought of what the space father had said. I was quiet for the rest of the day.

Once at the hospital, the doctor checked me over and said I was OK. I remember going home and lying down. The phone rang and it was my mother with bad news. My father was dying. He had lung cancer. He was scheduled to have a lung removed. She thought that I should get home to Ohio right away. He might not make it.

Without a moment's thought my daughter Renee and I flew back home from Alaska. At the time, it didn't occur to me that the place of the nuclear spill mentioned to me by the space man, was barely 24 miles away from my Dad's home in Parma, Ohio outside of Cleveland.

We returned to find my father in an extremely weak condition and needing a lot of care. My mother and sister were nearly worn out. Renee and I joined in and helped care for him. Eventually my mother thought I should take some quiet time out and see some friends. I'd been putting in some long hours. It had been a few months since my Dad's operation at that point.

I decided to go to a seminar at the Unity Church where there was going to be a guest speaker. I arrived a little early and ran into the speaker himself. He began by telling me he was going to be giving a talk on earthquakes that evening. I told him about my experience on Mt. McKinley in Alaska and how I'd been warned about an earthquake in Ohio.

It was time for the talk. I walked in and sat down in the audience. After a few other speakers, the gentleman I had spoken with earlier got up and said there a woman in the audience who had experienced a vision in the mountains of Alaska. I looked around and thought maybe someone else had had a vision in Alaska too.

Catching me completely off guard, the man called on me and asked me to speak. I was instantly not feeling so good. Suddenly, words started coming out of my mouth, "There is an earthquake coming to Ohio and a man in the Alaskan Mountains told me to warn you." Everyone started to laugh, so I stopped talking.

As if on cue, the lights went out in the church and a crack of lightning exploded outside.The church was dark for a few minutes. When the lights finally came back on, I heard a man's voice ask, "What did you say about an earthquake coming to Ohio?" Little did I know that a reporter from the local newspaper was there to report on the speaker's talk on earthquakes. The next morning it was all over the news, "Mystic Predicts Ohio Earthquake."

Here I am, my Dad is dying, and the television stations and newspaper are going nuts with the story. According to a comment by a local university expert, he thought I was correct on the possible timing of a rare earthquake, but that it would occur in an adjoining county. This made a lot of people question things. The company involved decided to move the nuclear waste from its position just off the lake. Evidently, it wasn't that difficult for them to move it off the water and back onto the land. And it was certainly better for public relations.

Within a few days the area in question was hit by a mild earthquake. You would have thought the world had come to an end. People came from all over. They were outside my house, standing everywhere. It was nuts. I couldn't stand it. Here I am, my Dad is dying, and people don't even care about what my family was going through. All they wanted was a reading or a healing. I decided I would leave after my Dad died. I was over Cleveland Ohio for good.

For the six months prior to his death, my father talked with me about my life, helping me prepare for his departure. As we talked and shared, his words repeated themselves, "Go west, Little Golden Bear. Seek out the traditions. Go back to your roots. I can't give you your destiny. I can't tell you what your vision is going to be. You must seek the elders for their knowledge," he said. "Go back to your roots. By going west, you will learn the truth. That is where you will find yourself." Now, as he lay dying, my father was sharing his beliefs with me. He told me of my Native American heritage, so that in those traditions I could find comfort and strength.

He knew that his death would leave a big hole in my life. His way to help fill that void was to help me find myself. Although my grandfather was taken from the reservation as a kid, spiritually it was always with him. His peoples' use of alcohol and drugs bothered him considerably.

As part of his preparation for death, my father requested a medicine pouch to ease the transition. White Wind, a Cherokee medicine man of the Turtle Clan, was called in. He was a retired police chief and a longtime friend of my father. Over those last days and after my Dad's death, he became an integral part of my life. White Wind, nicknamed Lucky, prepared the pouch that rested under my father's pillow. It wasn't until much later, after my father had passed, that I realized that Lucky was also preparing me for my father's death and preparing me to go on a journey. Lucky saw how badly I wanted to heal my father. Try to understand my perspective. I am a healer. I thought I could heal my father.

Now, as our family gathered in the small hospital room, I studied the face of this man I loved. Once a strong, tall, muscular figure, he now weighed less than a hundred pounds. Still, he was a handsome man. His dark hair and dark eyes had always turned heads when he walked into a room. Now with only one lung functional, every gasp reverberated throughout his body. His features were strong even though his body lay emaciated by the cancer.

I turned as my niece Kim came into the room. She carried one of my dad's "black" roses freshly picked from his garden. One of his true passions was his garden, especially his rose gardens. He had nurtured a special variety of deep blue "black" roses. They bloomed every five years. They had bloomed profusely the previous summer so no one expected them to flower again this year. By all accounts, they should be dormant. However, as my father neared death, his favorite roses opened into brilliance. Grasping the rose tentatively in her right hand, my niece approached him and placed it across his chest. My father reached up weakly and touched the rose, a slight smile creasing his face. Smelling the black rose, he turned to me, "Go west. Where you find your roots, you will find your peace."

"I will," I promised. "I will."

Watching his chest heave, it was obvious that his breathing was shallower and more labored. I knew the time quickly approached. I walked to the foot of the bed. My father liked to have his feet rubbed and by instinct I grabbed his feet. As I am an empath, at that moment I touched his soul. I think everyone has their own vision of what it's like crossing over. I felt surrounded by a mist. It was as if we were walking in the clouds, yet they had substance. I saw a lake ahead, clear in the distance. A bridge, a path over the light, oddly illuminated, stretched across the lake. Everywhere I looked I saw brother deer, the fox and the eagle. These were all animals that were important to my father.

As I looked ahead, I saw my relatives and friends who had passed on. I saw my beloved brother. I recognized a cousin, Charles, who had been killed during his service in Vietnam. I had always loved him and really wanted to talk with him. My Grandmother Edith was waiting with other relatives. I wanted so badly to reunite with all of them.

"No, Don't!" My father grabbed my arm and pulled me to an abrupt stop. I jerked back mentally and then looked behind me. My father was getting younger, looking as he had in his thirties and then his twenties. At his side walked White Wind, who was my father's friend and medicine man and teacher of the Turtle Clan of the Cherokee. He was a great medicine man.

"No, you can't go over there," Dad explained. "If you cross over, you can't come back the same way. You would have to rebirth." I had so many unanswered questions that I didn't know where to begin. I wanted to go with him. "No!" Uriah stated emphatically. "I have to leave you now. It's not your time."

I felt despair. Fear clutched at my stomach. My father, my security, was leaving and I wasn't ready. I thought that I could save him. As the thoughts of fear and failure raced through my mind, he read me one last time. He sometimes knew my thoughts before they crystallized in me.

"No," he urged. "You have to let go. You can't save me. You can't save anyone but yourself. That's the way it is. This is my path. I am dying to take cancer and self-hatred off this planet. Let me go, little one." His soft voice echoed in my head. "Let me go..."

"Look at your animal," White Wind instructed, his voice ringing deep in my ears. He looked through me, seeing my pain at my father's words. "Look at your animal."

My gaze shifted to the field beyond. A white buffalo lumbered along with a big black bear. There were three grizzly bears, white wolves and hawks. I recognized the white buffalo as my father's medicine. I knew that Lucky carried bear medicine. But what was my animal? I felt attracted to the wolves and I was aware of the power of the grizzlies. How would I know?

"You know which one." Lucky answered as if in response to my confusion.

I spotted a little bear cub. It didn't seem menacing like the others. It almost seemed lost, so much smaller than the rest. Feeling compassion for the underdog, I moved toward it, this little golden bear. This was my medicine, I knew it with certainty. I faced my father. He said," I'm sending White Wolf as your guide, to help you on your journey." I looked at him in wonder.

He said," You're Little Golden Bear. Now what do you seek? What will you learn?"

"What should I do?" I realized the significance of the medicine. The bear represents the healer on all levels. It can also mean you need to be healed. Was I a healer or do I need healing? Why was I a little bear and not a big bear? Not that it really matters. Little was OK.

In the vision, his hands held a prayer pipe. "You must take my pipe to the elders. They will show you what to do with it. Then you must seek your vision." he said. I touched the pipe, wondering if I would receive one. At that point in my life, I had no idea what being a pipe keeper meant. "You carry the buffalo and you carry the bear. Remember this, Little Golden Bear."

He went on, "You must let go of the Red Cloud and look for the White Cloud. There will be many horses. Look for the one horse and you will find the White Buffalo Calf pipe and your new life will begin." This was his message to me with his last breaths.

As to the meaning of these words, at the time, I did not have a clue. My father turned toward Lucky, nodding. Their eyes met in unspoken communication. "Lucky will take you back. Lucky, when she is ready to go west, give the sacred pipe to her to return to the elders. You know the rest."

"I don't want to go back. I want to go with you." I felt comfortable in that dimension. I no longer cared about returning to the earthly plane. "Please, let me go too. Don't leave me now!"

My father put his hand in front of my face as if to say "No, don't cross over." I smelled the black roses that were in this hand. The hand grew larger and larger, looming over me, mesmerizing me as the lines and definition of his palm took shape. Suddenly, I was back in my body. I opened my eyes.

"Dad?" I said. My father took his last breath. He was gone.

I could feel the ancient ones gathered around my family. I could feel them supporting us. With their power and strength surrounding me, I opened my mouth and the words poured out "Our Father who art in heaven." Much to my mother's surprise, I repeated the entire Lord's Prayer without consciously knowing the words. Then my chanting switched to a native tongue, again words I didn't recognize but whose meaning I understood in the depths of my soul.

I honored both aspects of my father's belief system, his native roots and the Christianity he later embraced at my mother's side. Up to the end, he wasn't a churchgoer. He always felt that his church was outside in nature. In his life, my father taught me to honor the earth and to live in harmony with all things.

In his death, my father taught me to connect with Spirit. I trusted Spirit. Now I would have to learn to trust myself.

Figure 1. Uriah, Cynthia's Father with pet fox, Pennsylvania

2
The Journey Begins

"Go west," were the most important words of my father's last talk with me. My father's death marked a new beginning in my life. The path of self-discovery began shortly after committing my father's bones to the safe keeping of Mother Earth. I then set off on a journey that would lead me from Cleveland to South Dakota, to return my father's clan pipe to the Lakota nation.

At some point during this journey I began to understand my father's dying words. I tried to return his pipe to the Lakota nation where I thought it rightfully belonged. They wouldn't talk with me about it or accept it back. I felt lost and confused. I didn't even know what the pipe meant. I was still hurting from my father's death.

When the elders of the tribe refused to talk with me I thought I was being rejected because of my rainbow-streaked hair, or because of my half- white blood. Later I found out I might have had better results if I had approached the elders in a more respectful manner. When I had gone to meet them, I had an attitude. I had arrived on a motorcycle wearing a biker jacket. But my attitude wasn't arrogance. It was anger. I wanted my father back.

I didn't know anything about the significance of the pipe until I met Chief Arvol Looking Horse. We met through a man named Chris White Cloud. Chief Looking Horse is the 19th Carrier of the White Buffalo Calf Pipe. He is a man with a lot of responsibilities.

My father's pipe was handed down from his father. According to my father, we are from the Hunkpapa band of the Lakota and descended from the lineage of the peace maker Sitting Bull. I later found out there are different pipes used for different personal and community prayers. In the Lakota Nation, all prayer pipes are dedicated to the spirit of the White Buffalo Calf

Woman. In other native nations, there are pipes with different stories and dedications.

Out of respect for my father, I learned the prayer pipe ceremony. The Lakota Nation call it the "chanupa wakan," or "chanupa," for short. The pipe taught me how to pray. We all need to learn how to unfold our own path in life. Mine has become a path of prayer but it didn't start out that way. In learning to pray, I learned to respect all living things. I pray with the chanupa in the morning and in the evening before dusk every day. In learning to pray, I learned how to honor the needs of the two-leggeds, the four leggeds, those that swim and fly and crawl, and all of our relations.

Prejudice comes in many forms. The chanupa teaches us to become one with the Creator, not just to live and take from the Earth. My prayer is, that one day all the people of this world will finally be at peace with each other. Then entire nations will smoke the prayer pipe together. I send my blessings to all of the prayer pipes on the planet.

> After visiting with the elders of my father's tribe in South Dakota, I moved to southern Colorado near the Ute tribe. I talked to Red Ute, a sundance chief. I stayed with the late Kaare Evensen Jr. whose Ute name was White Wind like my father's friend Lucky. Kaare was a good man and a true friend. White Wind told me about their sundance and said I would be a welcome supporter even though women were not permitted to dance in the Ute tradition at that time. I accepted his invitation to support and attend the Sundance in the future.

> I took numerous trips between South Dakota Sedona, Colorado and Sedona, Arizona and finally settled in Sedona. I did readings, healings and jeep tours of Sedona and the Grand Canyon. It was there that I met a man named Hollis Littlecreek, who became my spiritual teacher. Grandfather Hollis had a huge influence on me and had a lot to teach me about life.

> Hollis was a flute maker and he used to sell flutes at gatherings all around Sedona. I met him in front of the Circle K gas station. I was gassing up and we both went into the store at the same time. I paid for my gas and he bought a pack of cigarettes. We started talking about his flutes and he asked

if I'd ever been to the Coffee Pot for breakfast. He said it was the meeting spot in town. I knew it was just two blocks away so I told him I'd stop by sometime soon.

3
The Firewalk

The advantage, and the disadvantage, of driving across the country is that you get to spend a lot of time by yourself. In my case, the many hours of driving heightened my anger at my father's death and brought me face-to-face with my own fears. Feelings of self-doubt and unworthiness gnawed at me. What if I sought a vision and didn't find it, or didn't like it when I finally did find it? Was I really cut out for a life of service as a mystic or would I be better off finding a managerial job somewhere? Why did I always have to be the rescuer? Why couldn't I find a partner like my father, a man who was strong, capable and secure? What purpose did it serve for my father to die? A thousand and one questions and doubts tumbled over and over in my mind as if everything had been thrown into a massive blender and chopped up. It had been chopped until nothing was recognizable. All my thoughts had become an intermingled mush. By the time I reached Arizona, my anger had reached its peak. I was mad. I was scared and I was ready to explode.

Because there is no such thing as coincidence, I arrived in Sedona a few months after the time of the Harmonic Convergence. The Harmonic Convergence of August 16th and 17th was the world's first globally synchronized meditation based on the end of nine Mayan "Cycles of Hell." The Cycles of Hell began in 1519, the year that Spanish conquistador, Hernan Cortez, first landed on the Mexican Coast. Shortly thereafter he and his ship's crew, along with additional Spanish reinforcements, began to carry out a merciless genocide on the indigenous people of the region.

Astrologically, the Harmonic Convergence of August 1987 featured a grand trine of eight planets in late degrees of fire signs. At the time, I didn't know much about astrology but I knew that I liked what I saw of Sedona. The town bustled with activity as visionaries from around the world led ceremonies and workshops. This began months before and continued well after the actual Harmonic Convergence. Everywhere I turned, people were honoring this time of high spiritual energy with drum circles, and celebrations. I sat in on some of the workshops, drummed until my arms ached, chanted at the top of my lungs and explored the quaint streets. Later that summer I drove up into the hills, and sat beside a stream to gather my thoughts. Despite my many hours of chanting and meditation, nothing had reached the core of my pain over my father's death. I felt empty. I was beyond tears.

When I came down from the hills that day I stopped at the Coffee Pot Restaurant for lunch. I didn't know it at the time, but the Coffee Pot was a meeting place for many of the locals, spiritual leaders, music and t.v. stars and people you wanted to meet. It was the happening spot in town and still is. As I walked in, I scanned the huge bulletin board that flanked the entry. Notices of every sort and description were crammed onto the board. When I spotted a flyer advertising a fire walk, I ripped the whole thing from the board and stuffed it into my pocket. The fire walk was being organized by Larry Jensen, Michael BigBear, Todd Burke and Tim Heath. The thought of walking on fire fascinated me. I knew that my father had done it. I had seen it on television. I wanted to try it.

I couldn't sleep that night in my small tipi in Bear Canyon. (At the time, I didn't know its name was Bear Canyon – or the significance the bear was going to have in my life.) My mind wandered to the fire walk the next day. "Just once in this life," I thought, "I'd like someone to walk the fire for me. I'm tired of always being the strong one. I want someone to be strong for me." I fell asleep pondering these thoughts.

The next day, as I approached the fire walk site, I took in a view of the crowd. Some were obviously milling around, taking instruction, and waiting their turn. Others were onlookers, curious but not eager to go through the experience themselves. I joined the second group, close enough to see the glowing coals but not close enough to be tempted. I was standing near the end of the fire pit. Everyone seemed to be waiting. No one was walking across the coals quite yet.

"Little Golden Bear," a deep voice boomed out.

I was startled by the sound of my name and looked up. I was new in town and the people there didn't know me. Maybe I was mistaken or maybe there was another person there who shared my name.

"Little Golden Bear," the voice resonated across the hushed crowd. I quickly located the voice. A big man, tall and solidly built with dark hair and piercing eyes, stood out from the crowd by his size alone. "My name is Michael Big Bear. I'm going to walk the fire for you. I take the hand of Spirit. I walk on Spirit. I am Spirit."

Already barefoot with his pants rolled up, this giant man stepped onto the coals. The crowd waited expectantly. My eyes were riveted to his as I watched him cross the distance between us. His stride was not hurried, but strong and purposeful. When he reached the other side, he slowed slightly, then walked directly toward me. He bent down and scooped me up in his big arms, swinging me off the ground. I was really scared and struggled for a moment when, with his heart pressed against mine, he blasted me with such pure love that every wall came tumbling down. Tears spilled down my cheeks. The anger and fear that I had so carefully bottled up rushed out of me in huge sobs. No one had been able to reach my pain until this huge gentle bear shot pure love through my every defense. Safe in these arms, I grieved for my father, my brother, and my son that had died. Finally, after so many months, I was starting to release my anger at being abandoned by the men in my family.

Talk about instant manifestation! I wanted someone to walk the fire for me and I got it. Use your words wisely. Be careful what you ask for!

I have always been blessed with spiritual people in my life, people who are there when I need them. Michael Big Bear became a real friend that day, someone I could turn to when I needed advice. In fact, his compassion is so intense that he would show up today if I asked him to. Michael has always said," We are not here to change the world; we are here to change the way we look at it. Mother Earth has been here longer then us. She knows her needs." Thank you, Michael Big Bear. You are a true brother and will always be part of my family.

Figure 2. Michael Big Bear, Cynthia and Mayan Elder, Sedona

4
Meeting at the Coffee Pot

I'd been camping for a few days, hiking near Red Rock Crossing and Cathedral Rock. After a morning of meditation, it was time to return to civilization. I'd been hiking and meditating since sunrise. My stomach growled raucously as I gazed up. From the angle of the sun, I could tell it was probably about noon. Time to eat before my stomach scared away all the critters nearby. Reluctantly I stood and stretched. Reaching down, I pulled on my moccasins and trudged back to the car.

The road wound me around and out onto the main highway. Before I would stop to eat, I looked for the gas station where I had met Grandfather Hollis. I'd been riding on fumes for the last twenty miles. It's bad enough that Spirit had to do most of the driving for me due to my poor eyesight. I didn't want to tempt fate any further. Pulling into the Circle K, I pumped gas and walked up to pay. Seeing a sign for "FREE HOT DOGS" on the way to the window, I grabbed a hotdog, stopping only long enough for the ketchup and mustard. I stuffed it into my face as I walked.

"You eat hot dogs?" The young man who ran the cash register asked.

I looked at him in surprise. "Excuse me?"

"You don't recognize me, do you?" I looked at his face, the light brown hair, and his slightly uneven teeth as he smiled.

"Sure don't." I chuckled in amusement. "I'll eat anything when I'm as hungry as I am right now! So, who are you?"

"I saw you at the fire walk. I'm friends with Michael Big Bear and Grandfather Hollis."

I tried to place the young man at the fire walk, but everything from that evening was still a blur. We chatted for a few minutes until hunger overcame me again. I realized he was trying to pick me up and I needed to get lunch. With a wave, I headed toward my car. "I gotta go. I'm meeting Michael Big Bear at the CoffeePot and I think I'm already late. See you around."

I drove quickly to the restaurant. From the outside appearance, the CoffeePot was nothing special. It sported an air of small town meeting place, nondescript with a packed parking lot. There was no hostess to greet customers but at least there wasn't a line of people waiting. I walked into the main area, taking in the small tables and checkered tablecloths. My eyes moved from one table to another until I spotted Michael and Grandfather Hollis.

"Hey," I called in greeting as I walked across the room and slid into a chair. Michael greeted me with the same broad smile he greets everyone with, while Grandfather Hollis looked up and nodded.

"How come you order the same thing every time?" I joked with Grandfather Hollis. Every time we met at the CoffeePot, Grandfather ordered scrambled eggs. I wondered how many orders of scrambled eggs he had eaten in his life.

"You need to go into the woods," Grandfather Hollis responded, entirely ignoring my comment about the eggs.

"I just came from Red Rock," I said, referring to the time I had just spent camping.

"You think you're such a mystic," Grandfather Hollis said. You need to find and bring me back what I'm thinking of. It's in the woods. I don't think you can find it," Grandfather Hollis said, laying down the challenge.

"I'm sure I can," I countered, tossing my hair. I had found countless missing persons, I had seen earthquakes before they happened, and I had predicted world events. Why wouldn't I be able to find whatever object Hollis had in mind? That shouldn't be hard.

Michael watched our exchange in amusement. "Be careful, Blondie. Your ego is showing." Michael was the only person who got away with calling me Blondie.

"I surrender," I laughed. "I should learn not to argue with you guys. I don't have a chance. But I will have your object the next time we meet here."

"I'm looking forward to it." Michael winked at Hollis as he said it. "I think you may be trainable, if someone has enough time, and enough patience." Hollis and Michael laughed, exchanging knowing looks. I had known Hollis about a year. We had met on the Ute reservation. Michael had walked the fire for me only the day before, but already they were my teachers and my family. I settled back in my chair.

Since we had eaten at the Coffee Pot often, I knew the menu by heart. "A number twelve with bacon," I told the waitress as she approached with order pad in hand. "No water just coffee. Thanks." I handed the menu to the waitress and watched as my companions continued to eat their meals. I chatted aimlessly, often receiving no response from my companions. I got bored and started surveying the restaurant.

As I looked past Michael, my eyes were drawn to a nearby table. From the back, I saw a head of long blond hair and the broad shoulders. He was probably a handsome man, but that wasn't what caught my attention. On the back of his jeans jacket was the most incredible eagle I had ever seen, intricately detailed to catch the exhilaration of an eagle in flight. I stared at his back for a minute or two, completely taken by the eagle. Maybe because he felt my energy, he turned around. Our eyes locked. He looked familiar but

I had never seen him here before. There's no way I could know him. With his long blond hair and full, bushy beard, he gave the appearance of a mountain man. He wore simple clothes, a black tee shirt under his jacket and faded blue jeans.

With my eyes caught in his blue-gray ones, he smiled and motioned to the empty seat next to him. I nodded and walked across the room. As I approached, he stood up and offered his hand. "Hi, I'm Strong Eagle. Do you remember me from the fire walk?" His grip was firm as he held onto my hand.

"My name is Cynthia."

"I know, he said." His eyes bored into mine again. I had the eerie feeling that he was looking through me, past me. "You don't recognize me, do you?" he said.

I shook my head. He looked so familiar but I still couldn't place him.

"Cynthia, you know me as Shane."

How did he know my name? I hadn't told him and we hadn't met before.

Instantly I was transported to my childhood in Pennsylvania. Images of Shane floated like a vision, almost a hallucination through my mind. Racing over the hills, running through the meadows, two young children, hand in hand . . .

"Hurry up, slowpoke I want to show you something." With a toss of his blond hair, Shane ran at full speed ahead of me. I watched his faded overalls bouncing along the overgrown path until his shaggy locks totally disappeared. Of course, with my eyesight, that was easy. All that someone needed to do was move ten feet from me and the person escaped my range of view. It was no wonder that I was known as "the half-blind half-breed."

"Slow down," I yelled. He knew I couldn't keep up.

Sometimes being in a physical body was a real pain. I would never be able to run as fast as I wanted to. I decided to take my time, to stop and play with the dandelions and buttercups that lined the trail. Why did people think of them as weeds? With a prayer of thanksgiving for their sacrifice, I stooped to snap the stems of the delicate plants. My father and mother had taught me to honor all forms of life as part of our tradition.

Even before I understood the importance of Mother Earth in sustaining all life, I felt the universal connection. More than anything, I loved playing outdoors, feeling the Earth underneath me, supporting me. When I was trapped inside a house or school, I felt confined. Walls closed in, suffocating me. I loved the freedom I felt outdoors.

Shane shared the same love of nature. That's why we had been best buddies. After picking and arranging a bouquet of dandelions and buttercups in my hand, I skipped down the weed-choked path looking through the dense undergrowth. Where was Shane? Was he hiding from me again?

"Look up, silly," he shouted. I looked up. Shane was perched in the branch of an old oak tree, one leg hanging over each side of the branch. "Join me." He patted the bare limb next to him.

"No way!" I said, shaking my head quickly from side to side. "Come down and play with me or I'm going home." I pretended to pout and started to turn away.

Shane shimmied down the tree and appeared instantly at my side. I never got used to the fact that he moved so fast. He grabbed my small hand and started to lead me down the path. "I have something special to show you."

We walked silently, the sun shining brightly on our faces, the path growing more indistinguishable. Finally, through the dense brush, we came across a clearing. As we approached, I gasped in surprise. There stood a shell of a house, its charred remains standing ghostlike against the dark pine forest behind it. There was something frightening and yet compelling about it.

"This is where we lived. Come see my room." Shane pulled me reluctantly forward. He climbed over a blackened beam, still hanging onto my hand. "This was my room." He surveyed the burnt timbers proudly. I couldn't even tell where the walls had been but obviously he saw the room from memory. His reality was different from mine but I could look inside his head and see his room as he remembered it. "We lived here until the fire killed my parents."

I nodded. I knew he had died in a fire. I felt its heat when I walked through him the first time. You see, I could never tell the difference between a real person and a spirit by looking at someone, because my vision was so poor. I knew spirit because I could walk through their bodies. That's how I knew Shane was in spirit. As a kid, I envied his freedom. He could move very quickly and never get tired. Later I learned that even spirit had limitations. When I played checkers with my grandfather, who was also in spirit, I had to move the pieces for him.

"I'm going to have to leave you soon." Shane's words broke into my reverie. I turned toward him, dropping my dandelion bouquet as I whirled around.

"Are you going on vacation?" I asked.

"Not really. I'm going to be born but we'll meet again in the red mountains

"Okay," I replied, not really understanding what he meant. I wasn't prepared when a few days later Shane disappeared from my life. For years I wondered what he meant and where he had gone. I looked all over Pennsylvania for red mountains thinking I might find him. I never found him until today at the Coffee Pot in Sedona.

"Have you been up into the mountains?" Shane asked, breaking into my trek down memory lane. "Not really." I answered. "'I'll see you again in the red mountains." That's what you said to me before you left."

"And you understand now."

I nodded in agreement. Shane provided the confirmation I needed. When I had driven into Sedona for the first time, the energy felt right. Surrounded by red sandy mountains, the town was nestled in a beautiful valley. It was known as an agricultural center and became an artist's community and a metaphysical retreat. Later, after the Harmonic Convergence, it became a popular tourist attraction. Due to its immense popularity, the town of Sedona was growing very quickly, with new construction sprouting up on every street. I hesitated to fall in love with the town, not because of its obvious attraction, but because the earth was being thrown into constant turmoil with the growth. Yet, I felt pulled by the town, by its energy.

"Go west." The words echoed in my head as I sat next to Shane and stared at the grease-spattered menu. Shane and my father had played critical roles in my childhood. Now they merged again, in a different place. When my father told me to go west to find myself, I wondered how I would know where to go. After all, the west is a big place. Now I knew I was in the right place. The rest was up to me.

Meeting Shane was the beginning of my shaman's journey, with Shane as my shaman brother. Strong Eagle taught me to love myself. He helped me to always love unconditionally. He taught me that the act of unconditional love is freedom. He is truly Strong Eagle, now known as White Bear. He is one of my best friends and forever my brother. Thank you, Shane.

My vision had manifested itself. Eagle represents illumination. My name, Little Golden Bear, means healing. Shane illuminated my path and was the light that led me to my yearlong vision quest. That vision quest led me to find my spiritual self, my true home. To Shane, these words say it best:

Love is patient, Love is kind, Love bears all things, hopes all things, Love never fails.
I Corinthians

5

The Search

A couple of days later I headed toward Sacred Canyon, now known as Boynton Canyon, with determination as my companion. I didn't know exactly where to go to find the mystery object Grandfather Hollis had in mind, but the canyon seemed as good a starting point as any. There were plenty of woods there. I would find his object. I knew I would. I just wish I could have cheated and read his mind at the restaurant. He must have deliberately blocked me.

I pulled into one of the many rough-hewn trails leading into the canyon and parked the car. Parking was free back then. Now you pay a fee to hike or visit the sites. Reaching into the back seat, I pulled out my moccasins and backpack. I put on the moccasins, shouldered my backpack and set off on the trail. I walked all day, stopping occasionally for water and rest. I stopped and looked at trees, thinking that maybe Hollis had a leaf in mind. Nothing felt right. I scoured the ground for plants, thinking that maybe I was supposed to bring back a special herb. Again, nothing felt right. On the trail, I met a coyote. I struggled to recall what I knew of coyote medicine. Coyote was the trickster, the master of illusion. With coyote, things were never what they seemed to be. How did that apply to my situation? I had lots of questions, but no answers.

As evening approached, I felt tired, discouraged and very hungry. I had hiked all day with nothing to eat. I was deep in the woods and going deeper.

Because I had intended to find the object quickly, I didn't pack food. Yet I refused to go back empty-handed. I wouldn't leave until I found what I came to get.

Taking the bend in the trail, I came upon a group of people, longhair hippie types. I recognized them immediately as Rainbow Children, part of the many groups that had converged for the Solstice Celebration. They were camped alongside a stream with a few tents and miscellaneous camping gear.

"Hey, are you hungry?" a bearded guy called out. The night shadows danced across the landscape as their campfire glowed before me.

"Starved," I admitted. "I've been walking all day. I forgot to bring food."

"Come, join us. We're leaving tomorrow. If this food doesn't get eaten, it'll spoil."

I didn't have to be talked into staying. Joining them immediately beside the fire, I filled up on the vegetables, cheese and the bread they offered. My stomach appeased, I sat back and listened to their stories and shared some of mine. As darkness descended, the campers urged me to spend the night with them. I crashed in one of their tents, thankful for the shelter. They gave me a blanket and the next morning insisted I keep it. I still have it to this day, a gray fleece with a white star on it.

The next morning when they broke camp, I took off in the opposite direction. Part of me wanted to leave the woods, to return to my car and civilization. The stubborn part took over. I refused to admit failure to Grandfather Hollis. I didn't want to admit defeat. So, I trudged on, looking right and left for something, anything, picking up stones, kicking at the dirt. About midmorning, I met a guy on the path. He was somewhat small, light brown hair, dressed in jeans and a tee shirt.

"Hi, there," I greeted him.

His eyes met mine. He nodded in greeting.

"Where are you headed?" I asked, trying to engage him in conversation.

He pointed toward a hill in the distance.

"What's wrong with you? Can't you talk?" I blurted out. This was one of those times that I didn't think before I spoke.

He shook his head no. Then I felt terrible. This guy was obviously a deaf mute and I had just stepped all over his disability. 'That was a good job Cynthia,' I chided myself. 'You just got a lesson in sensitivity.'

"What's your name?" I asked, more gently this time.

He picked up a stick, drawing in the dirt. LIGHT, he spelled out.

"Your name is Light?" I asked. He nodded yes.

Then he motioned that I should join him as he started to walk away. I deliberated a moment. After all, I was on a mission. Watching his back as he moved further away, I reached my decision. I wasn't having any success finding what I came for alone, so what did I have to lose? I started "following the Light!"

I caught up to Light and walked alongside him on the trail. We hand-signaled to each other: communicating as we went. The distant hill was now in front of us. Light searched through the brush and handed me the perfect walking stick. Then he started to climb.

Because I didn't know what else to do, I followed him upward. I noticed we were climbing Chinly Rock. For almost an hour, we worked our way slowly upward, grabbing onto roots and branches for support, walking when we could, half-crawling through the rough spots. When we reached the top, Light didn't stop. He walked over to the edge of the cliff and motioned to a ledge below.

He wanted me to climb down to the ledge. Before I decided whether to climb down, I suddenly saw my car in the distance. I realized I had hiked in a circle toward the place where I had started. Now looking down into the hole of Chinly Rock the three storey drop off terrified me. I shook my head and mouthed the words "No way!" Just looking down, I was petrified. After my near brush with death in my car accident, I wasn't in any mood to put myself in danger. There was no way I wanted to hang over the edge. I had climbed many mountains around Sedona and in the West but nothing like this one.

"Come on," he motioned.

I stood rooted to the spot.

"All right," he shrugged. "I'll go without you." He started to climb over the edge and down into the hole without the help of climbing rope or gear.

 I ran to him and grabbed his sleeve. "I'm coming," I said as he turned toward me. "Help me get my feet onto the ledge please."

With Light holding onto my jacket to stabilize me, I lowered myself carefully to the narrow ledge. As soon as I was safely standing there, he lowered himself beside me and sat down.

"It's too scary to try to sit down," I said inching my foot along the one-foot ledge. With his face turned away, Light ignored me. Finally, I gave up and lowered myself to a sitting position, keeping my back pressed against the wall of the ledge. My feet dangled over the side. The red sandstone was so brittle; it could have broken off at any moment.

"It's beautiful!" I exclaimed trying to distract myself from my fear as I watched hawks and ravens circling nearby. We were so high up that as I looked down toward the ground, I realized we were on their level! Suddenly, just as I was starting to relax, I felt wings brush against my hair. I screamed as two bats flew past me.

 "It's okay," Light reassured me, signaling with his hands.

 I checked my hair. Was it true that bats dive-bombed humans? Would they continue to come after me? 'All right, get yourself under control,' I urged myself. I tried to relax again and took a few deep breaths. I didn't see any bats circling for the kill.

I remembered something my father had taught me. I could hear him in my head "If you fear it, it will hurt you. If you see its worth, it won't." I surrendered to the bat's beauty. It eased my fear.

"Look," I said, grabbing Light's sleeve as I pointed toward a raven that appeared to be circling us. I remembered the message of the Raven. Raven is the messenger of magic. It signifies the beginning of a change of consciousness. Native teachings say that the color black is not evil. Black can mean the seeking of answers, the void, or the road of the spiritual shadow. Raven is the guardian of ceremonial magic, guiding the healing and the change of consciousness that will bring about a new reality and dispel "dis-ease."

"Look," I repeated as I tugged insistently.

"Be quiet!" he signaled.

How bad is that -- to have a deaf mute tell me to be quiet! Light ignored me then as he closed his eyes in meditation.

I sat on the ledge, then, totally silent. I even stopped swinging my feet. Because they were so close, I concentrated on the ravens. I watched as their wings fluttered slightly and then glided. As I concentrated, I started to feel their motion, to feel the air as it brushed past the feathers, to feel the slight shifts in wind currents. Before I knew what was happening, I was flying, circling with them, noiseless and free. I was a raven.

When I finally returned to my body, I was standing at the bottom of the hollow inside of Chinly Rock. From up above Light laughed and smiled at me as he looked down from the ledge. I have no memory whatsoever of climbing down. Seeing daylight ahead of me, I waved goodbye to Light, walked out of Chinly and hiked quickly back to my car. I was surprised at how close I was to the car. It felt like I had been wandering for days.

The next day, I went to breakfast at the CoffeePot and ordered scrambled eggs and bacon, the favorite meal of Grandfather Hollis. Sitting back in the corner alone, I watched quietly as people entered and left the restaurant.

When Grandfather Hollis came in, he headed directly for me. I continued eating as he walked over.

"Good morning, Little Bear," he said as he sat down.

I nodded and continued eating.

The waitress came over and Grandfather Hollis ordered. He settled back in his chair and observed as I ate. For five minutes, we sat in companionable silence, not saying anything. His breakfast arrived and Hollis dug into his food. When he finished, he picked up his coffee cup and sipped. I doubt that I had ever been quiet that long in my life. You see, normally I love to talk, that's my nature.

"I see you finally found what I was thinking of," Hollis said.

"Yep," I answered with resignation. Instead of feeling pride at my success, I felt intense humility. I had ventured on a mission, not realizing that I was really searching for myself. I was privileged to learn from a patient and wise teacher.

"Good. Now you'll always know how to go home to yourself. You have learned the wisdom of silence."

I nodded. Through silencing my chatter, both external and internal, I had found peace. Grandfather Hollis stood up, nodded, and left the restaurant, a slight smile dancing across his face.

Hollis Littlecreek was my most important medicine teacher. He taught me about the pipe, the flute, silence, and the sweat lodge. He taught me and supported me as a sundancer. He passed on April 30th, 1999, on my Dad's birthday. He was a great teacher and a great friend. He is missed and never forgotten. Thank you, Hollis.

Figure 3. Elder Hollis Littlecreek, Sedona

6

The Prayer Pipe

The next time I saw Grandfather Hollis, he was carrying his familiar pouch. "I have something for you," he said. He reached inside his pouch and rummaged around for a few seconds. Finally, his hand tightened around the object. "Here, I made this especially for you."

My eyes brightened as Grandfather Hollis placed a necklace in my outstretched palm. I turned it around in my hand and looked up into his eyes. The necklace was made from beads of many colors, red, yellow, blue and so on. In the center dangled an ivory carving of a wolf. I slipped the necklace over my head, noticing that the pendant fell just above my heart. "Thank you, Grandfather" I said.

"You're most welcome, my dear. Learn from it."

"This means a lot to me," I said as I continued to examine the necklace. I fingered it as I spoke. I knew Grandfather Hollis had undoubtedly carved the wolf himself. Like many of the elders, he was a talented artisan. "I can't imagine when you had time to do this. I know you've been busy making flutes."

Grandfather Hollis nodded slowly. "You make time for the important things in life."

I reached out and hugged him, kissing him lightly and reverently on the cheek. I loved this dear old man; he was like a father to me. As he held me close, I realized how much I missed my own father. Tears welled up in my eyes. It was taking me a long time to adjust to my father's absence. I missed his wisdom, I missed the way he listened to me and seemed to understand what I wasn't saying as well as what I did say.

"Thank you for the necklace," I said between tears. "I will think of you as I wear it. You are an incredible teacher."

At the time that I spoke those words, I had no idea how true they were. A few days later, I found out that Grandfather Hollis had made necklaces for other women. All their necklaces were comprised of the same multicolored beads interspersed with seashells. I was sad. Why didn't I get a necklace like theirs? Why was mine different? Didn't I deserve the same necklace as they did? As I look back now, I realize that I didn't have a clue. I was saddened and failed to see the honor that he had shown me. It was a long time before I realized the true meaning of the white wolf on the necklace. Hollis knew immediately why it took me a yearlong vision quest to discover who I am. I am at heart a loner and a deep thinker. I am White Wolf.

I don't know if it was part of my grieving process over my father or frustration about my life in general, but I became extremely agitated about staying in Sedona. When Shane suggested a trip to Colorado, I readily offered my new red Honda Prelude for the trip. I was ready to leave Sedona even though I had only been there for a short while. What I didn't realize was that Sedona, and the intense spiritual energy of the place, puts every personal issue directly in your face. Whatever was unresolved came to the surface. It was time to leave.

A few days later, Shane, better known as Strong Eagle, arrived. I packed our belongings and we headed for the mountains. Shane brought his wolf, Wolfa, along and we were going to visit friends and stay with them. Prior to the trip, Shane had been working on an alabaster and ivory pipe. I had been carving my own pipe. At his death, my father had instructed Lucky White Wind to make me a pipe. And he did, but it was a bear pipe of the Cherokee, not a Buffalo Calf Woman pipe. So, too impatient to wait, I made my own. Shane laid his white buffalo pipe next to mine on the back seat. He was proud of the pipe; it had turned out very well.

Shane drove for a while and then I drove. When we stopped for gas, Shane took the wheel again because I'd become sleepy.

"I'll drive the rest of the way," he said. Relieved, I leaned back against the seat and immediately fell asleep.

My shoulder crashed hard into the door. I awoke to the sensation of spinning. It felt like my head was going in one direction and my body in another. From nowhere a cold wind rushed in. The air screamed like a jet landing! I awoke quickly, but to what? The seat belt grabbed me, trapping me like a vise. There was an eerie silence. From behind me, I felt Wolfa's nose nudge up against my neck.

We were upside down in the car. The back window was knocked out. The front end was caved in like a truck had run over it. "Shane? Open the door!" I said about three times. From the corner of my eye, I saw him move beside me. Blood trickled down his face from a cut on his forehead. "What happened?" I asked.

I took off my seat belt and reached over to help him unfasten his. He had been knocked unconscious. I was relieved he could talk. "I don't know," he said. "Let's get out of the car."

By the time we freed ourselves, Wolfa was outside waiting for us. "Wolfa," I cried. "I'm so glad you're okay."

We walked away from the car, struggled to the road, and looked back. My new Honda was twisted into a grotesque shape. Our pipes were lying outside the car on the opposite side. The rest of our belongings were still inside the car. When the police arrived, we learned that we were in Wolf Canyon near Pike's Peak. We were lucky; we had walked away with no physical injuries except Shane's cut. My car, on the other hand, was not so lucky. It didn't take an insurance adjuster to tell me it was totaled. Shane had fallen asleep at the wheel and had driven off the road. He had run the car up a tree and flipped us over onto the hood. Since we were on the side of a mountain, it could have been worse!

The next day, I sought out a Lakota teacher in Manitou Springs. I brought my battered pipe, with its horns falling off and its stem broken from the crash. The elders looked at me and remarked, "This girl has got a lot to learn." From them I learned that pipes were made of red stone, not alabaster or ivory. Shane and I had tried to emulate the tradition, without understanding it. I had grown impatient and decided to make my own pipe rather than wait for White Wind to make it.

"Little Golden Bear, you need to bury this pipe" said this man of honor. I knew I couldn't dispute his teaching, but I felt bad about burying the pipe. I walked around for a long time looking for exactly the right place. After a lot of tears, I wrapped the pipe in red cloth, with tobacco and sage. Next to a big tree, I dug a hole and gently placed the pipe in the earth.

A grandmother walked over to the tree and invited me into the unipee lodge better known to some as a sweat lodge.

"I can't do a sweat with you," I replied, full of humility. "I dishonored the pipe. I'm not worthy of the circle." The grandmother advised me to use the unipee lodge anyway as I might find it beneficial.

As I approached the lodge I saw my friend Leonard Crow Dog. Leonard had been in Ohio years earlier. He had done a rain dance for some local farmers that my father and I had attended. It promptly rained hard. I was impressed. Leonard didn't remember me. He seemed to remember some of the story and didn't really care. That was the past. His concern was that we know the truth and honor it. I could feel his love and his wariness. I understood.

Stories are great teachers. I'd like to explain what I got from these stories. During my time with Leonard, I learned about White Buffalo Calf Woman.

One of the traditions associated with the Lakota, Dakota, and Nakota nations is to tell the story of the White Buffalo Calf Woman.

White Buffalo Calf Woman is believed to have appeared to the tribes nineteen generations ago, bringing instruction on how to do the sacred ceremonies and on how to live a life in balance. She left behind a sacred bundle containing the sacred pipe of peace. It was one of the seven sacred gifts she gave to the Nations. She left many prophecies about the time that she would return in the future. The birth of the white buffalo calf named Miracle, in Janesville, Wisconsin in 1994, is believed to have been the first sign that these times are at hand. There is much more to the beginning and end of this story. I feel that the story of the White Buffalo Calf Woman should be told in a sacred circle, in a sacred way.

I learned about the Elk family. For many generations, the head of the Elk family kept the pipe for the Nation. Today, one of the prayer pipes is now in the hands of one of the Looking Horse family. I learned about these families. They all have their stories. I learned not to judge them. That was the lesson for me. Different families tell different stories. I've seen white families do the same thing. It makes me laugh and warm inside to know that we are all related. I hope that one day, nations around the world will see this truth, and will come to respect each other. I believed that in the year of 2012 peace would begin to come to this Earth. It would be accompanied by chaos, like birth, but it ushers in a time of peace.

The next day, I was presented with my first pipe along with a group of other initiates. In the Lakota tradition, it was made of red stone. The bowl represents the female; the stem represents the male.

"This is your pipe." I was told. "Pray with it. Learn from it. Don't let others smoke it for a long time. If you do, they will become your family and you must always pray for them." The elder Lone Wolf explained further, "Smoke tobacco or mixed herbs from the grandmother."

I remember hearing my father talk about his pipe. He had it for a year before he used it. Obviously, I had a lot to learn and a lot to think about. The name Lone Wolf was inscribed on it. While I noticed the name, it did not truly register at that time that my medicine animal was the wolf too, the white wolf.

This was the first pipe I was to receive. The second pipe came a few weeks later, from White Wind (Lucky), a Cherokee medicine man of the Turtle clan and a great friend of my father. He was worried that the Lakota would not help me. He knew they didn't like the fact that my father had left the reservation, never to return. He also knew they were not particularly fond of mixed bloods It was my father's wish that I receive this second pipe, a Bear pipe. I knew I would learn from it.

The bear pipe had been carved in the Cherokee tradition. "The black bear is for healing, not for yourself, but for others. You must use this pipe for healing only and not of yourself. This is the pipe your father wanted you to have."

My thoughts went back to the pipe I had tried to make for myself, because I was tired of waiting for White Wind's pipe. Tears of shame flowed down my face. Already I had dishonored the tradition.

"Don't cry, little one," Lucky said gently. "You are learning. The medicine path is not always easy. Sometimes we want a huge lantern to light the way. You have to learn to travel by the light of the firefly."

I held the pipe in my hands, and turned it over. As I flipped it back over, Lucky continued. "With this pipe, you will carry your father's buffalo and my bear. When you pray with this pipe, your prayers shall be for others. Take it with you on your journey." He gave me very old tobacco in an old leather bag. The tobacco had been his great grandfather's. His great grandfather had grown it.

Each pipe marked a phase of my journey. I carry the first pipe, a white buffalo calf pipe, to teach that life is a prayer of thanks for my every moment. Also, it is not a privilege to carry a pipe. It is an honor. What I mean by that is that I received the pipe to learn how to pray to Great Spirit. It is a sacred tool. The purpose of the second pipe is to pray for others on the journey home. Both pipes have been blessed.

White Wind's words ran again through my head, "This is your personal pipe. Don't use it in public unless you are asked to do so by Spirit or an elder. Pray for the ones that ask you to and pray for their families."

I have kept that vow. Thank you, Spirit. Thank you, Elders. Thank you, Lakota nation. Thank you, Lucky. Thank you, Father. Bless you all.

Figure 4. "Lucky" White Wind, Cherokee Medicine Man, wearing my Dad's necklace that he later gifted to me.

7
Coincidence

After we crashed my car in Colorado, I decided to go back to Cleveland and visit my family. I had received a call that my psychic abilities were needed. As I traveled cross-country, I realized that I was still grieving my father's death and unable to come to terms with it. I missed him terribly and I was angry that he had left. I found myself caught in a spiral of sorrow, anger, and disbelief. I knew that my emotions were all part of the grieving cycle, but that knowledge didn't help. It had been a year but I still hurt.

While I was in Cleveland, Lucky White Wind contacted me. "I need to see you again before you leave," he said. I didn't realize that I was going any place. At that time, I had no special plans. "You're not done yet. Your journey has only begun. You still have to go back to your roots," Lucky replied, answering the questions in my mind. "Your father wanted you to go west to find your roots. That's where you belong. You have much to learn from the Native tradition."

"How will I know what to do?" I asked.

"You must go on a vision quest. Seek the tradition. Listen to the elders. Find Your path."

A couple of days later, Shane called. "When are you coming back?"

I laughed. Obviously, everyone knew I was going back out west but me.

Within days, I was headed back out West. I flew to Colorado where I met up with Shane. He picked me up at the airport in an old, green pickup truck. "Bought this baby cheap," he said, thumping on her dashboard. "She's seen a few miles, but she's still got life in her." I looked at the dents in the side of the door, the rear fender that was hanging at an odd angle, and there was a spare tire mounted on the front.

"What's the tire for?" I asked innocently. "Is that the spare?"

"No, that's our brakes, in case the others don't work." Shane laughed as he replied.

I thumped the Michelin tied to the front bumper. "You've got to be kidding!" He wasn't. I have seen a lot of old beater trucks in my life, but this one won the prize. I threw my suitcases in the back and pulled hard on the door handle.

"I have to open it from the inside," Shane explained as he climbed into the seat and reached across to the door handle. "It's temperamental."

I slid into the seat. My hands wandered to the tattered upholstery, slipping my fingers into the cracks in the seat. "These cracks could almost be dangerous. This one here kind of looks like the Grand Canyon," I said jokingly. I thought of my shiny red Honda with its perfect seats. I had decided not to replace it.

We stayed with Raymond, a friend that lived in Manitou Springs, near Pikes Peak. He lived alone and had a few extra rooms. His brother was a teacher at Case Western Reserve back in Ohio. Shane and I decided to stay a few days.

Next door lived a man who had the habit of drinking heavily and beating his dog. I felt bad for the dog, tied up all day. After witnessing the abuse heaped on this animal, I made it my mission to free him. He was a mix of red wolf and Norwegian elkhound. I called him Bear Bear and Bear for short. I often fed him and let him off the chain for a while.

One morning Shane suggested "Since it's early, let's get started today." After packing my gear, I gave Bear one last breakfast, stroked him, and let him off his chain.

I got in the truck. Shane gunned the accelerator and we took off. "My parents are expecting us in a few days." he said. I looked back at Bear. I expected to see him hunched where I had left him. He was bounding down the road after us. We slowed down. He caught up with us and jumped in the back with Shane's wolf, Wolfa. He quickly sat down and stared straight at the road ahead. He didn't look back.

"I guess Bear is coming along," I offered. Shane shrugged, "I think he's chosen a better life." I learned from that wolf.

8

The Cascade Mountains

As we traveled across the mountains from Colorado to Washington, I took my turn driving. Because the brakes didn't work very well, we had to use low gears to travel down the winding hills. I quickly learned to appreciate the signs alongside mountain roads, which urged drivers to use low gear. We had no choice! Besides, the slower we went, the smaller the jolt when we had to use our Michelin "bumper" to come to a full stop.

When we arrived in Washington, a year had passed since my father's completion. As we traveled across the mountains, the need for a vision quest became clear to me. I needed to take a year to find my Native roots, to seek my vision. I had the blessing of Grandfather Hollis, I had the approval of my family. I was ready. Just as meeting Shane was no coincidence, it was no coincidence that Shane's parents owned land in the Cascade Mountains that adjoined national forest land. Shane and his father fixed the brakes on the truck. Shane took me hiking in the mountains. He showed me the many streams he crossed and the many paths that he had hiked as a child. His love of the land made him shun the comforts of city living, preferring the beauty of life in the wild. As I watched the glow on his face, I came to understand the heart of this mountain man.

One day, I found the perfect place for my quest. It was a cave, hiding in the side of the mountain, surrounded by large trees overlooking a meadow. "This is it!" I declared as I stood at its entrance.

"Are you sure?" Shane asked.

"Positive," I replied. "This is where I'm going to do my vision quest."

Over the next few days, we returned to the cave, taking a few belongings and spending time preparing it. I put the propane lantern and cookstove in one corner, set up a cot in the other. On our way up, we passed an area where people had dumped things. I scavenged an old door and a bunch of wood. There was even a fence roll that we threw into the truck. With Shane's help, I built a hut of sorts inside the cave. It even had a door, the one we had scavenged from the dump.

"Cynthia, are you sure you want to do this?" Shane's mother asked one night as I was making my final preparations. "That area is totally wild, you know. You'll be up there alone, no civilization for miles, just all kinds of wildlife."

"I know. I spent a lot of time outdoors with my dad. I'm not afraid."

"I don't know, a young woman alone..." her voice trailed off.

"I'll be okay. Shane will come up sometimes when he's not working."

"Still, it's not very safe," she persisted. "There's been trouble, talk of trouble."

"What kind of trouble?"

"There are Men, alcoholic mountain men. They live up there, folks never see them. But sometimes they come down, beat on women and rape them. There's been talk around town." She seemed hesitant to say more, because I blanched visibly. Rape was one of my issues, something I had not worked through. Memories of being forced flooded over me. I felt hot and cold at the same time. I took a deep breath.

"I need to do it. I'll be fine." I tried to sound convincing, but I'm not sure I was successful.

"Just be careful," she said.

I nodded. Of course, I would. I would be as careful as a person could be, under the circumstances.

Figure 5. Cynthia and Shane below the cave and waterfall, Cascade Mountains, Washington

9

Firewood

I moved to the cave forty-five minutes north of Shane's parents place, in the mid spring. Within a few days, I was becoming accustomed to my new home. Shane was working at a logging camp a few towns away from his parents' place. He would come up and stay with me on occasion when he was off work. I was alone for the most part, working with the land. Bear, my half-wolf half- Norwegian elk hound was my constant companion along with Wolfa. She was totally mesmerized by Bear. He was constantly at her side. And both wolves usually hung close to me. Whether I was planting my garden or gathering wood or herbs, Bear and Wolfa hovered within earshot.

I knew it was important to prepare for winter, so I spent a great deal of time working the soil and planting crops. As the vegetables started to grow, I realized that porcupines, squirrels and rabbits were eating them as fast as they came up. I spread wolf hair around. I planted marigolds and a few herbs most animals don't like. I had to protect them. I unrolled the fence and propped it up with sticks. I even constructed a gate, so that my wolves could come and go.

I settled into a daily routine. Every day I got up early, meditated and prayed. As part of my ritual, I was building a medicine wheel to symbolize my journey. To build a medicine wheel takes 365 days. I found a level space on top of a hill. From this vantage point, I could see for miles. As I hiked the land, I gathered rocks and crystals for my wheel. As spring merged into summer, my medicine wheel started to take shape.

I worked on the cave. I added a porch onto the front of it. Shane constructed an outhouse, his idea. He helped me with it when he came up. He was an expert with a chain saw. He cut a half moon out of the door so I could see out.

Life was challenging but fun. Some days I worked in the garden, pulling weeds and thinning the plants and watering. Other days, the dogs and I took walks. I gathered herbs and porcupine quills, along with other things that would be vital to my survival in the coming months. I took my axe with me and cut down dead trees. Later I returned and dragged them to the cave where they fell victim to my chopping block for firewood. As I spent more time outside with the wild animals, I found my senses becoming more attuned to every sound. I heard Shane's truck when he was still miles away, right after he pulled into the winding and twisted lane that led up the mountain. I could hear the clang of his loose bumper and doors as he climbed the steep hill. My sense of smell heightened so that I could smell and hear just about anything before I saw it.

One day, as I was chopping wood, I heard a truck coming my way. I knew it wasn't Shane, I could tell by the sound. I continued chopping as the truck came into view. I looked up to see a man. From my viewpoint, I saw his bearded face and flannel shirt. The truck edged closer and stopped. A big man, tall and obviously very strong, climbed out of the pickup. The warnings about mountain men beating and raping women sounded in my head.

"Why are you chopping wood?" He didn't greet me or ask my name. He got right to the point. He walked over to my woodpile, stacked neatly just outside the cave entrance. He picked up a piece of my freshly chopped wood and held it in his huge hand.

"For the winter," I replied. Part of me struggled against stating my intentions to spend the winter on the land.

"This won't burn. It's still too green." With those words, he started to throw my woodpile in his truck. The hours of hard labor won out over my fear. I saw my efforts disappearing.

"But..." He stopped and looked at me.

"I'll bring you some wood that will burn in return for this wood. This needs to season." He swung back around and continued to throw pieces into the pickup. In his mind, the issue was obviously settled.

I shrugged. Since he pointed it out, I knew he was right. Most of the wood came from trees I had just chopped down. It was still green. As I watched, he finished loading the wood, climbed into his truck and headed off in a direction further up the mountain. I didn't know his name; I didn't know where he lived. And even if I had, what was I going to do? Call 911 and report a wood thief?

A few days later, I heard his truck again. As I watched, he pulled alongside the cave. His truck was loaded with wood, darkened from sitting out in the weather. It was obviously seasoned. Some of the chunks were quite large and would have to be split. Without a word, he climbed out of the truck, unloaded and stacked the wood. He turned to go.

"Thank you," I called after him. He grunted in response. Then he started his truck and disappeared, going back up the mountain. I never learned his name or said more than a few words to him. But, I learned an important lesson from him. I trusted my instincts with him and they were right. He did exactly what he said he would do.

Some people, when they read this story, will wonder why he didn't just bring wood to me, why he took my wood first. After all, I was a young woman and very green myself. It would be a somewhat natural instinct to protect me. To understand the scenario though, understand that the people of the mountain. There is an unspoken respect for another being that is living and surviving on the land. If he had brought wood to me without taking mine, it would be demeaning, undermining my ability to take care of myself. By taking my wood, it became barter, my wood for his. Both of us maintained our independence and our dignity. His actions were rooted in respect and trust.

I knew that the people of the town were a little worried about me, especially those that had talked with me. Most of them thought I was nuts, and the story of me cutting green wood didn't help.

They knew I had wolves and that I was going to live in the cave for a year, one way or another. However, this mountain man didn't hang around town. His homestead was even further up the mountain than mine. He probably had not heard the local gossip about the crazy wolf woman who lived in the cave. He didn't question my existence, but certainly questioned my survival techniques.

By bartering wood, this giant man taught me a good lesson on trust. He taught me to trust my instincts, my inner knowing. We all need lessons on trusting our inner voice. All too often, the noise of the outside world drowns it out. We can't hear it through the barrage of noise. Everything else clamors for our attention and our inner voice gets subdued, lost in the cacophony. Living alone for a year amplified my inner voice as if I had a microphone attached to it. Since then my inner voice comes through loud and clear. I just have to listen to it. Thank You Spirit and although I'll never know your name, mountain man. Thank you for your unconditional concern for a neighbor.

10

Confronting Fear

This day started as any other. At sunrise, I was up and out on a short walk with my animals. Then I started splitting wood. I brought fresh water in and threw the old out. I had to clean up after the wolves and myself daily or the cramped living quarters would have become unbearable very quickly.

With the heat of the sun as my companion, I worked on the woodpile all morning, stopping for occasional water breaks. The wolves were enjoying the weather, playing with each other and then running off into the woods. It was peaceful and quiet.

The peace was broken first by the sound. As I mentioned, my senses had become acutely tuned so that I sensed changes well before they happened. That's what happened this time. I heard and felt the hooves striking the ground before I saw the horse. I smelled the rider, a mixture of alcohol, cigarettes and stale sweat, before he rode into view. I became instantly alert and looked around for my wolves. They were nowhere in sight. Because I smelled him before I saw him, I knew that he was an alcoholic. I also knew that alcoholics were violent and unpredictable. My worst fear was materializing before my eyes.

As a younger woman, I had been raped. Even though it happened many years ago, I was still traumatized by the memory. While he rode into view, flashbacks of my rape experience flooded me. Memories of the past intermingled with the present. It was hard to separate the past and the present as I watched this large, unkempt man approach. Terrified as I was, I vowed never to feel as helpless again. Gripping the ax tightly with my right hand, I bent down and grabbed a piece of wood with my left. I stood with my legs firmly planted as he rode nearer. No matter the circumstances, I was not going to show the fear I felt.

He stopped a couple of feet from my fence. He dismounted, stumbling as he hit the ground. The horse bolted slightly, jerking his head against the reins.

"Stop it, dumb ass," the man cursed at his horse. He raised his hand as if to strike it with the leather reins.

I peered into the widened eyes of the horse, the whites growing larger by the second. I felt pity for this gentle animal, forced to serve this excuse for a human being. I held his eyes, communicating silently. "It's okay," I soothed. "We all know who the ass is. Settle down. He's not worth it."

The horse nodded slightly. With my coaxing, the horse regained control of his fear. He slowly lowered his head and began nibbling at the grass. I turned my attention to the man as he walked forward and fumbled with my gate. He flung it wide-open and stepped inside. He had already invaded my space. My hands gripped my weapons more tightly. I was determined not to show fear.

"What the hell are you doing here?" he growled. "You don't belong here."

"Excuse me. I'm a friend of the owner of this land. I'm staying here," I replied simply. He stopped five feet from me. At this close distance, his stench was overwhelming. The smell nauseated me. I fought to keep my breakfast down.

I couldn't help but observe the results of years of alcohol abuse. Skin fell around his face and neck in folds. His brown eyes were overshadowed by the creeping jaundice, becoming a collage of yellow and red. It was impossible to determine when his clothes had been washed last. From their appearance and odor, it was obvious that he had passed out and wet himself at least once since his last change of clothes. While I felt disgust, I also felt pity.

"You don't belong here," he continued again. "This isn't your land, wolf woman."

"I'm leasing it." I kept my answers short and concise. Meanwhile, I kept looking for my wolves. They usually stayed close enough to protect me.

"Then you have to tear down this fence. It's keeping my cows from getting to the water."

He ignored the fact that there was an easy cow path which went around the fence to the water. He was very angry. He walked toward the fence and yanked on one of the tree poles supporting the fence.

"Stop!" I commanded. "Just leave. I'll move the fence."

His hand stopped. He turned toward me. The hair on my arms stood up as I registered his menacing look. "Who are you to..."

A roar from behind me drowned out his words. I suddenly saw my wolves encircling the area. Bear appeared beside me and growled, his teeth set in a snarl. Totally frightened, I reached down to touch Bear as I whirled around to find the source of the roar.

A mountain lion was crouched on the grassy knoll above the cave, her body sleek and muscular. She looked poised to pounce as she threw her head back in another roar. Without thinking, I moved closer to the mountain man as if seeking his protection. Terrified of the lion, I kept my eyes glued to her, expecting her to attack at any time. I didn't like my alternatives, raped or eaten. Two of my worst fears, staring me in the face at once!

As quickly as she had appeared, the lion turned and ran off. I edged away from the man, Bear at my side and Wolfa and another two wild wolves still circling. The unwanted alcoholic visitor glanced around, sizing up his chances against my wolves. He was badly outnumbered. Angry but resigned, he walked through the gate and toward his horse. I latched the gate behind him. From his mount, he yelled at me "You're one messed up girl, living with wolves and lions. You are not wanted here. Get off this land. If you don't keep your wolves off my land, I'll kill them." With those parting words, he slapped his horse and thundered away.

I yelled back, "Bite me," thinking like my wolves. I didn't know what I was saying. I was more afraid of the mountain lion than the man at the time. Looking back at my cave, I shuddered. The mountain lion was gone. My wolves had run off too. I wanted to go into my cave but I was worried. I didn't want to get too close, in case the mountain lion had gone inside.

"What should I do?" I said aloud. "I'm screwed. I can't go back to the cave. I can't stay here. What if the lion comes back?" I paced back and forth. I felt trapped and confused.
Before I realized what was happening, my feet carried me toward my medicine wheel. Once I arrived, I sat down in the middle. At first, I nervously watched for the lion. Once I started praying, my mindset changed. I felt safe inside the sacred space. I prayed for a couple of hours, chanting and singing.

As I was placing a stone in the southwest of the medicine wheel several hours later, I heard spirit say to me "You need to build a unipee lodge." I remembered I had written a few notes in my journal about the last sweat lodge I had experienced. I had also brought a few books on Native tradition that I thought might help. I forgot my fear of the mountain lion and went back to the cave with thoughts of the lodge.

11

The Lodge

Looking through my books, I found one on sweat lodges. I felt ready to build one now, just as Spirit had suggested. I was excited about all the pictures of finished lodges but I didn't have a book that showed me how to build one. All night I thought about it but I remained clueless as to the actual construction. My idea had become a source of frustration. "Great," I chided myself. "I can't even build a lodge."

While I was doing my chores the next day, I heard Shane's truck. A half-hour later he arrived. He and a native woman named She-Bear bounced out of the truck. "We came up to check on you," Shane declared. "Are you okay? We heard that you were threatened by some guy."

"I'm fine,' I replied. "It was scary. He was drunk and nasty. But he didn't want to tangle with the mountain lion. She backed him off.'

"So, he didn't hurt you?"

"He didn't have a chance," I confirmed. "He was more scared than I was."

I found out that the mountain man had been at the bar spouting his mouth off about the "crazy wolf woman". My friends heard about it and thought that they had better check on me.

Once they realized I wasn't harmed, we started discussing my real concern, how to build a lodge. Shane knew a lot about lodges and so did She-Bear. She was a Washington Indian: I can't remember the name of her tribe because I wasn't into names back then. I was concentrating on survival.

They agreed to help, so together we walked down to the stream for some willow branches for supports. I had a lot of blankets for the walls. Shane and She-Bear said, "We need to dig a hole for the fire pit in the center of the lodge and we need to dig a fire pit on the outside to heat the rocks before we bring them in."

She-Bear showed me how to make prayer ties for the lodge. A prayer tie is filled with tobacco and covered with fabric in one of seven colors for the seven directions. She-Bear had met some of the Lakota in Oregon at the Sundance and remembered some of the things they did. She told me to put the door in the east, the direction of the Eagle, illumination and beginnings, even though her people didn't do it that way.

We gathered lava rocks for the fire. We called the rocks "grandfather rocks." Lava rocks are volcanic. When they're heated, they maintain the heat for a long time and rarely explode. The rocks are integral to the sweat lodge. Rock people are record keepers. They release legends and stories as they heat and cool. I found forty rocks that day, perfect for my lodge.

Now with the new firewood, I was ready to do a sweat. I gathered up some sage and sweet grass. Then I prepared my prayer pipe, and my drum for the lodge.

I waited for sundown to use the new lodge. Since it was getting late, She-Bear and Shane got ready to go. I thanked She-Bear for her help and gave her a round blanket I had made. I gave Shane a medicine bag that he had always admired.

They offered to inform the ranger station on their way down the mountain that I would be doing a lodge this evening, or in the morning. In the mountains, there was always concern about wildfires, so informing the ranger was important.

It was around five in the afternoon. I got my fire pit together; I think my wolves thought I was going to cook something. I placed the lava rocks in the outside fire pit and laid out the branches to build the fire, blessing it with tobacco. I went into the lodge by getting down on my knees and crawling in backward. Since the purpose of the ceremony was purification, I was symbolically leaving the old life behind. I lit sage and smudged the space inside.

I made the prayer ties for the lodge. The ties were composed of seven colors. Yellow was used to represent the east and the eagle, the beginning of something new. The red was for the south representing the wolf and coyote as teachers. Black is for the west. It is symbolized by the bear and by the feminine healing energy. In the north was white, inextricably tied to white buffalo, my father, gratitude, and wisdom. The blue represented sky and everything above. Green stood for mother earth and the plant kingdom. To honor Spirit, I chose purple for the center within because I was new to the ceremony and not sure what color to use. I prayed for help from Great Spirit. I had a lot of purifying to do!

A half-hour later, I came out and went to the stream to fetch water. I placed one bucket inside filled with cool, clean water and a little drink dipper. To make sure that I didn't let the fire get out of hand, I dug the hole near a fifty-gallon blue drum filled with drinking water that Shane had brought me. I think that's why we picked that place for the lodge. He'd put the heavy water drum there and he wouldn't have to move it. I fed the wolves and watched the fire, singing a few songs, and feeling great.

When the rocks were heated, I grabbed my shovel. I carefully lifted them one by one from the fire, carried them into the lodge and put them in the hole in the center of the lodge. I placed seven rocks in the middle for the first round. She-Bear had instructed me to do four rounds of seven rocks each. After I placed the grandfather rocks, I asked for their guidance. I wasn't sure where to sit. I figured that by the time I did four rounds, I was sure to find out. So for now, I closed the flap and plopped down on the ground just inside the lodge.

The lodge was dark and comforting, like being in the womb of the mother. I sat in silence, throwing herbs and water on the rocks and watching the stream spray up. I started to pray, thanking the spirits for the day. Suddenly, my heart flew open and released all kinds of feelings. Before I knew it, the rocks were cooling and the round was over. I had made it through the first round. I sighed in relief. I realized, though, that I had forgotten to ask spirit how many grandfather rocks to use for the next round.

I crawled out of the small door. My heart throbbed. I went over to the fire pit and decided to use ten grandfather rocks in the second round. After all, I had a lot to release. I wanted to get it all out.

When I pulled the door flap and sat down inside, the heat of the ten sacred stones filled the tiny space. I put water and herbs on the rocks and the steam immediately filled the lodge. I felt choked. I couldn't breathe. I coughed, steam filling my lungs and setting them on fire. I was still lucid enough that I contemplated opening the door, although I couldn't see it. It was so hot that I was afraid I would die or burn up.

I lay down and started to cry my face dangerously near the heated rocks. I cried to the mother, then the father, then my grandmother, my grandfather, and my children. I performed "poor me" like no one else could. I was an actress and the lodge was my stage. I cried until no more tears would come. It was like having dry heaves. I lay on the ground, exhausted from emotion. I think I passed out for a while.

After an indeterminate time, I finally composed myself and reached out to open the door. The cool air rushed in, reviving me. I crawled out slowly and tried to stand on unsteady legs. In the bright starlight, I decide to walk to the steam and thought seriously about jumping in the water. Instead, I sat down on the bank and dangled my feet in the water. God, it felt wonderful. My cheeks still burned from the heat and my lungs felt seared. I quickly splashed cold water on my face. I cupped my hands and brought huge handfuls to my mouth. Finally, my body stopped burning and I felt refreshed as I slowly inched my body into the cool water.

I thought about the next round and wondered what I should be doing next. I laughed to myself," I'm not even sure if I'm doing this right. I almost killed myself the last round. God, what could be next?" I thought back to She-Bear's instructions. I heard her voice," After the second round, bring your pipe in. Pray with it and learn from it."

After having ten rocks almost kill me, I was not sure what the pipe would do. I knew from my father that smoking the pipe was powerful. In that moment, I realized just how much I had to learn! Somewhat reluctantly, I pulled my feet from the stream and walked back to the fire pit. I stirred the fire, grabbed my shovel and carried five grandfather rocks into the lodge. I didn't want to over do it again.

I decided to sit in the West Side of the lodge. I poured a little water and herbs on the grandfather rocks. By now, it was dark outside and the lodge was pitch black. I had to feel for everything in the dark, fumbling around for the prayer pipe. I filled it with tobacco and started to smoke. I felt good, like everything was right with the world. I placed the pipe between my legs and stared at the glowing rocks.

When I looked up, an Elder was sitting across from me. I hadn't heard him enter, but I was not surprised. "What's your name? Who are you?' I asked. Maybe I was being impolite, but I like to know who's sharing my space.

He gazed at me and pointed at the water. I handed him the dipper full of water. As I watched, he poured it on the grandfather rocks and started singing songs. I closed my eyes and listened, transported by the melodic chanting. As quickly as it began, the singing stopped. I opened my eyes. The elder was gone but the voice lingered in the air. I still heard him singing.

Across from me in the darkness appeared a white wolf. His hair was long and flowing. "I am your guide. I will be helping you," the wolf explained. Then White Buffalo Calf Woman appeared. Dressed in white leather she sat in front of me, the wolf next to her. She told me the stories of the pipe. It was a little different than the stories I had heard from the Lakota. I was wondering why she had come to me. I talked with her for a few minutes. She told me what was going to happen in the next millennium. She told me many stories I do not wish to repeat right now.

"I have a big question,' I said, knowing that our conversation was coming to an end.

"Yes?" she asked. Her hands were folded in her lap as she waited patiently.

"When my father died, he asked me to return this pipe to the Nation. I tried, but they wouldn't take it. Now I don't know what to do with it."

She seemed to be lost in thought, but only for a moment. "You must bury it, here in the mountains." She replied. "When the time is right, you may come back for it, if you choose. This is an ancient pipe belonging to a specific clan. All the elders who have smoked this pipe have passed on. As she explained many more stories I was starting to understand that this was a prayer pipe.

I didn't understand everything, but I trusted her words. After all, her words were spoken in the lodge, in a sacred space. She told me many stories of the people. I listened attentively, trying to understand them. At one point, I asked her who she was. She answered, "Some know me as White Buffalo Calf Woman, and others know me as someone else."

As quickly as she appeared, The White Buffalo Calf Woman left. I figured that the round was over, so I lifted-up the door and crawled out. As I looked up at the stars, my heart felt peaceful for the first time since my father had died.

I had one more round left. I prayed and asked the grandfather for the number of rocks I needed. Spirit answered, "Three." I grabbed the shovel and dug three more rocks out of the fire. I crawled inside and crawled all around the lodge, in a clockwise circle until I arrived back at the door. I pulled the flap closed, placed herbs on the rocks, and sprinkled water on the grandfathers.

The final round was my thanksgiving round. I gave thanks for the lessons that night and for nights I knew would follow. Even though my father's spirit hadn't touched me like I had wished it would, I felt his guidance. I didn't know for sure that I was doing the Lakota lodge right, but I was doing the best I could. Spirit honored it because it was from my heart. I felt clear, clean and renewed.

The fire went out late that night. There was a bright moon, almost full. My wolves were howling at a coyote in the distance. Back at the cave, I cooked my dinner over the glowing embers and ate it ravenously. I felt satiated in many ways. Peace had burrowed its way into my heart, filling me with joy. "Thank you, Spirit. Thank you for helping me find the path. Thank you, White Buffalo Calf Woman. Thank you, Father."

I walked back to the lodge and looked around to make sure the fire was out. I was smiling. That night I slept like a bear, under a buffalo robe with the wolves at my side. All was right with the world.

Later I found out that you don't leave the lodge between rounds if there is more than one person doing the purification ceremony. Typically, one person stays outside the lodge during the many rounds to tend the fire and put the rocks into the lodge fire pit. It is ok however, to leave the lodge between rounds, if you are alone.

12

The Medicine Wheel

Because I wanted to learn as much as possible, I spent a lot of time reading about many Native traditions. Prior to setting up camp on the mountain, I had decided to build a medicine wheel as a calendar for my 365 days. In addition to building my garden, I committed myself to creating a medicine wheel. I was not sure if the Lakota used one, But Sun Bear, a dear teacher from Washington that visited Sedona, taught me how to do it. I thought I would honor him and it would help me.

During my first week on the land, I discovered the ideal spot. My wolves loved to hike. On our morning hike one day, we found a huge hill. The top of the hill was flat and open. It was close to the cave. I could see the front door of the cave and could make it there in a few minutes if I needed to. There were a few trees, but for the most part it was barren. I fantasized that I was on the top of the world because one could see for miles. This was going to be my medicine wheel area. It was a special place. It would mark my journey and my quest.

Every day I trekked up the hill and placed a stone on the medicine wheel. I planted tobacco, sweet-grass, sage and mullein in the wheel. As I prayed, animals came by to visit. I got in the habit of taking along the blue corn that my Hopi mother, Anita Polacca, had given me.

On one occasion, a porcupine came to visit. Normally I would have been scared because I certainly didn't want to get stuck with quills. "Hi, there," I said. The porcupine stopped and stared at me. "Don't be afraid. I promise I won't be either." After that, the porcupine came to visit almost every day. He also helped me dig around the medicine wheel. He seemed to like cleaning as if he wanted to help me keep the medicine wheel in good condition.

One day he came close enough for me to touch him. I found that you could indeed pet a porcupine. I recommend doing it very carefully, with a down stroke. He would leave a few needles here and there, especially when the wolves came around.

It was funny to watch Wolfa. She'd been hit with needles from another porcupine a month before meeting this one. She wanted to fight with him. It was great to watch her heal. If anything, they became friends and on occasion, he would even come into the cave. One day he even crawled up onto my lap and fell asleep. To this day I have some of those needles and I remember him. In case you are wondering I named him Needles.

As I built my medicine wheel, I continued to read about the four directions. The East shield was the Eagle. The Eagle stood for illumination and clarity, something I needed in my life. In the South, the shield was White Wolf, and to some, Coyote the trickster. White Wolf brought the teaching and the clarity of truth to the circle. In the West was Bear. It represented healing, introspection and goals. As far as I could see, that was the purpose of my vision quest. In the North was the White Buffalo. Because of my father, I was very familiar with the legend of the White Buffalo. The White Buffalo is sacred and represents peace, love, wisdom and gratitude. The White Buffalo Calf Woman brought the sacred ceremonies to her people, and the teaching of the prayer pipe to teach them how to pray. I had already put the four directional stones in my medicine wheel and every day I was now filling in the spaces between them with the other stones and by doing daily prayers.

Over the summer, I spent a lot of time at the medicine wheel. I usually did my prayer pipe there at sunrise and sunset. It was a peaceful place to meditate and pray. I was amazed at how quickly the wheel started to take shape.

One day, my wolves were being particularly playful. I decided to skip gardening that day and take a long hike. I packed water, jerky, and some apples that where growing wild nearby.

"Come on, Mom!" the wolves urged. "Don't be so slow."

"Give me a break!" I countered. "I've only got two legs. There's no way I can keep up with you." I was at a point that I could understand my wolves as they bantered with me.

As we walked, we got further and further away from our camp. I suddenly realized that I was lost. I didn't have a clue how to get home. We kept walking, stumbling upon a clear, pristine waterfall, running over stunning black rocks. It was so beautiful. I sat beside the water and watched as my wolves ran in and out of the water, jumping and playing.

I'd never been able to see well in a creek bed. The sunlight is reflected off the stones and the water in such a way that it leaves me feeling unstable. I usually carry my walking stick for support. Just like kids, they kept urging me to join them. With my eyesight, or lack thereof, it scared me. The water was deep and dark. I chickened out. I walked around the rocks and found a sign saying: "Keystone Park Area". I didn't know where that was and I had no map with me.

"Oh well," I thought to myself, "On to a new journey." I followed the trail and found a road sign. That was great. I had found a road but I didn't know where it went. Finally, I whistled to my wolves and they came running. "Let's go home. It's time for dinner," I urged.

Truthfully, I couldn't get home without them. I had no idea where the cave was or which direction to follow. I could see the sun was going down, but couldn't tell from which angle.
Strangely though, I wasn't concerned. I knew that the wolves had an excellent sense of direction and wouldn't leave me stranded.

Suddenly, two hawks flew by, almost as if they had come to get us. As they circled overhead, I started to walk down the road and the wolves followed. "Okay, let's go." The wolves stared at me, not moving. I implored, "Please take me home." Wolfa understood. She took me home to the cave as a-crow-flies, the shortest way. That is not necessarily the easiest way. It was bush wacking! I covered up my hands with my jacket to keep them from getting scratched. I had to keep up with the wolves as they crashed through the bush and over creeks and up and down steep hills before we finally made it back home. I had cuts on my legs and arms from crashing through the brambles. This was the hardest part of the journey. I found an easier way back later. What had taken us all day to hike on the way out took only a fraction of the time to get back.

By the time we got home, it was after dark. I made dinner for all, making sure to honor my hawk friends. I cut off a piece of the animal I was cooking for the wolves and myself and threw it to the two hawks outside the cave.

It was a quiet night. All the wolves were sound asleep. I knew I would be the one on guard that night. I learned that day that the wolves love me and see me as one of their family. As I drifted off to sleep, a white wolf crossed my peripheral vision. He seemed real, sitting in my cave, staring at me. I wondered if the hawks really had come for us.

The medicine wheel is traditionally started in the middle of spring and continues through the summer, fall and winter. I made the wheel in a little less than 365 days. My east shield was the Eagle (Illumination/clarity), south shield white Wolf (Innocence/ inner child,) west shield Bear (Introspection/Goals,) and north shield White Buffalo, (peace, love, wisdom/gratitude.) In the center, I had built a fire pit and when I was not using it I placed a large crystal in the center, along with sage and sweet grass that I picked on the journey up the mountain. I replanted sage, sweet grass, mullein and seeded tobacco on the hilltop. I placed a new stone in the circle every morning. When the snow came, I would place the rock people in a small circle in the cave and take them up to add to the wheel when I could. The medicine wheel was my calendar. It was showing me where I came from, where I was going, and most of all, where I was.

Figure 6. From top left: Dad with pet fox, Cynthia and Claudia on steps, Cynthia, Claudia and Dad at the beach and Cynthia with horse Brandy Kai

Figure 7. from top left: Aerial shot of cave (red arrow) Close-up cave, Cynthia & Shane at cave waterfall, Insert-wolves

Figure 8. Cynthia in cave with loft bed, shelves for supplies and mirrors to catch & reflect sunlight, Bottom left: Wire spool table from Nostradamus vision, Insert: Cynthia's cave cat Snowball

Figure 9: Left to right: Cynthia with wolves Buddy Beau and Buddha, Sedona

Figure 10: Cynthia feeding Rainbow Spirit grain hay treats, Grand Canyon area

Figure 11. top: Cynthia and Charles first meeting with the White Buffalo, bottom left: Cynthia and Charles in Bend, Oregon and bottom right: Jim and Cynthia, Grand Canyon area

13

Preparing for Winter

With the passing of the seasons, I prepared for winter. I harvested food from my small garden, drying it before storing it in containers. I hung herbs in the cave, enjoying their aromatic fragrance every morning as I awoke. As the days shortened and the sunshine dwindled, I spent more time inside and less time outside. Like a bear, I was preparing my den for winter. I even had some honey in the larder I'd built to keep the bugs out.

When the first snowflakes fell, I decided it was time to stock up on the supplies I couldn't grow. I had already stacked everything from the garden onto makeshift shelves. I set aside the extra food I had grown to take into town with me.

It was part of my belief that I needed to not touch money for a year. I felt that I needed to remain "clean" of the world's influence. I would use the extra food and beaded medicine pouches I had made with herbs inside of them to trade for the staples I needed. Everything would be purchased by barter.

Early one morning, I walked toward the old green truck Shane had left for me and whistled to the wolves. "Want to go to town today?" I called out.

Bear and Wolfa ran up to me, nuzzling their heads against my hands. "Want to go to town?" I repeated. While I had always talked to my animals a lot, I realized that I was now talking to my wolves about everything. It was amazing how a few months spent alone had changed me. My wolves had become my best friends.

"Yeah, it sounds great," they answered in unison. Of course, others might not have heard their voices, but I did. I slapped the truck bed with my right hand. They leaped up, running in small circles and panting with excitement, their nails grating against the battered truck bed. Raising the tailgate with my left hand, I tied it in place with twine in my right hand. "You guys settle down," I scolded like a mother. "Jeez, I can't take you anywhere."

I climbed into the truck through a window. The driver's door latch didn't work so I had tied the door closed with twine. A large towel covered the big spring that popped up in the middle of the seat.

I drove slowly down the dirt lane until I came to the descent. Since I had little brakes, I kept the truck in low gear, letting the drag of the motor slow down the rate of descent. By the time we reached town, I had a headache from the high-pitched whine of the motor and from coming down the hill at 50 miles an hour with no brakes.

I pulled into a parking spot. Luckily this town didn't have parking meters, just horse posts for tying up horses. I bumped against the post, using the old tire tied to the front of the truck as a brake. It was a good thing that this small town hadn't adopted parallel parking – I would have had to hit another car to stop! I slid out of the window. Bear and Wolfa didn't wait for me to lower the tailgate. They jumped over it and onto the street. A couple of people on the sidewalk glanced skittishly in my direction. They walked quickly toward the hardware store and practically ran inside.

I don't know if people in town were more afraid of me or of my wolves. I must have been a sight. My hair flew in different directions, tied back with a headband. I looked down at my old, dirty jeans. There wasn't an easier way to wash clothes up in the mountains. I had to carry water from the stream, build a fire, and then heat it. Besides, who cared? My wolves sure didn't mind. Sometimes washing clothes was just too much work to bother.

I later learned that the townspeople called me "the crazy rainbow wolf woman". They also called me "The woman who runs with wolves". The book of the same title had just been released and it became an easy title to pin on me. While I only came to town a few times during my year in the mountains, it seems that I had gained a reputation.

Because I hadn't been off the mountain for six weeks, I reveled in the feel of the town. God, I missed people sometimes. I felt a physical hunger for human companionship. I wanted to stay in town for a few days, soak in a hot tub, talk to anyone, watch TV, guzzle ice cold beer, and eat until I couldn't move. At this point I was down to 100 pounds and a bit weak. I wanted clean sheets, clean clothes, and a clean body.

I forced myself back to reality. Dark clouds hung in the sky. The air smelled like rain, or even worse, snow. I didn't have time to dawdle. In the mountains, snowstorms sometimes strike with ferocity. I had to get my shopping list done.

I walked into the small store carrying the medicine herb pouches I had made and my excess vegetables. I bartered for everything I needed. I traded my handiwork and labor for staples such as flour, corn bread mix, sea salt, baking soda, sugar, olive oil, candles, propane and other necessities. During the summer, I had even traded for a chain saw and leather that I would use for making winter boots. I also traded two tires for a hand sewing machine that could sew leather. Knowing that I wouldn't get off the mountain for a few months of winter, I had to make sure that I had everything I needed. After I selected my staples, I spied the Snickers bars. Believe it or not, they were being sold in boxes of fifty. I grabbed two boxes and the clerk threw in one extra bar for good measure. 101 Snickers bars...a title of a movie, perhaps?

"Here, take these," the clerk handed me a small jar of dried mushrooms. "They'll be good on salads." She also gave me some bones for the wolves.

"Thanks. They'll be a nice treat," I said as I stuffed the jar in with the rest of my purchases and whistled for my wolves.
I met up with Shane's mother Ellie. She came to help as I was loading the truck. She gave me yarn to make my round blankets some fabric for sewing, patches of leather, and a few books. She also brought me a Christmas present. She had sewn me a beautiful jean jacket with a golden bear on the back and a heart on the front. The buttons were made of old buffalo nickels.

"I love it," I cried in delight. "Thanks!" She was a fantastic seamstress. She could sew anything. She made kites that were awe-inspiring and sold all over the U.S. She also made full-sized teepees. There wasn't anything she couldn't make. She was a real Earth mother.

She smiled. "Are you sure you want to stay up there all winter?" Her eyes mirrored her concern. I wondered if she knew something that I didn't.

"I'll be okay," I said, giving her a hug. "Really."

She reached into a plastic bag and pulled out a box. "Well, you might need this. I know you love those 2000 piece puzzles."

"I sure do," I confirmed.

Wolfa was already in the truck. Bear jumped in and we headed back up the mountain as light snowflakes whirled around us. We made it back with no time to spare. The first snowstorm of the winter was already blustering outside. As I tidied up my cave home, I listened to the wind howl. The snow was drifting, half way covering the door already. It was going to be a long winter.

All summer, I had been preparing for this. I didn't really know what it was going to be like, spending a winter alone in these mountains. I tended to my personal necessities first, setting up a bucket in the corner of the cave to be used as a toilet when it was just too cold to go outside. I had come across an old discarded toilet in the woods. I considered bringing it inside until I realized that there wouldn't be any way to empty it. Caves rarely have running water, at least not on command. A bucket made more sense.

As the daylight shortened and the growing hours dwindled, I spent more time inside. I was already feeling claustrophobic in the cave. It was dark and dreary. I knew I needed something to break up the darkness but I didn't know how to create more light. It was a cave, after all.

I decided to put in windows. I dug holes on the north side and surrounded them with old boards I found lying around. Then I covered each hole with a piece of rounded glass, using mud as a mortar. Lying in bed at night, I looked out at the stars through my makeshift windows. Their beauty was awesome. I felt proud of myself. As the nights consistently dipped below freezing, I brought my herbs inside and continued to grow them with the help of the natural light.

It wasn't until winter struck full force that I realized what an idiot I had been. I opened a window and the fierce northern winds blew out the glass. I nearly froze my butt off. I tried six times to pack dirt around it and reframe it. Finally, I had to give up. I put a bear hide over the hole and boarded the whole thing up. Always protect the north side from winter winds. This was a lesson I learned too late.

I hiked in the woods often that fall. On my hikes, I usually found something. Someone had thrown away a sink and a counter, so I dragged them back to the cave and pushed them up against the wall. My cave was furnished with other people's garbage, things that others had tossed. They became my great treasures as I set up shop. I have great issues with people spoiling Mother Earth and trashing her natural beauty. From another perspective, their waste supported me for a year

One day I found a little propane stove that was probably thrown out of an RV. There was nothing wrong with it. It worked fine after I cleaned it up. Somebody probably got confused and pitched it. I found plates, cooking utensils, cups, pots and pans. I even found a bathtub.

She-Bear's quarter horse and an old draft horse had wandered up the mountain and onto my place. They later towed the bathtub to my front door. I fed them and held them till their owners came for them. She-Bear was so happy. She was becoming a good friend. Finally, the mountain people were starting to see me as a person who could take care of herself, even though I was probably their entertainment, "the Rainbow Wolf Woman."

She-Bear started checking in on me and sending supplies that I might use. Her ranch was at least fifty miles away. Mountain people take care of each other while trying to stay out of each other's business.

With the heat of summer gone, it had gotten too nippy to enjoy the mountain stream. Before winter set in, I decided to treat myself to a hot bath. I found old cement blocks to set the bathtub on so I could build a fire underneath. To fill it, I ran a hose from the stream. I put in rose hips and lavender oil that had been bartered in one of my trades. I set up the hose and siphoned water from the stream until the tub was almost full.

Then I built a small fire and sat back to wait, occasionally checking the water temperature. When it finally felt warm enough, I stripped off my clothes and climbed in. I concocted this incredible fantasy that my true love would discover me and we would live happily ever after...

I was just settling in when I realized that the tub was scorching my skin. The porcelain had gotten very hot from the fire underneath and was burning my behind. I jumped back out of the tub. Another lesson learned. Heat the water, but not IN the tub! My luxurious bath had turned into a blistering experience. I had nearly made soup out of myself! It was a month or so before I took a bath again. I put the tub in the back of the cave so I could heat the water and take a real bath.

Out hiking one day, I came across a dump. There were old cars, tires stripped off, and fenders missing. There was lumber, doors and parts of a house. I found a small dining room table that I brought back. Lying in one corner was one of those spiral wheels that are used to hold cable wires. It was big and round, with a hole in the center. I rolled it to the cave and it served as a desk. The bottom was rounded like a mushroom but I could put my feet on it. It fit my body perfectly for a writing table.

My greatest find was three huge mirrors. At first, I didn't know where to put them. It wasn't like I wanted to stare at myself. I soon realized that they made my small home feel more spacious. I put the first mirror above the window and hung the second across from it so that natural light was reflected off the ceiling.

In the center of the cave to support the ceiling, stood a big tree beam, about seven feet tall. Because the wolves kept pestering the lynx kittens that had come to live with me, I decided to make a tree house for the cats. Using the tree beam as the base, I attached branches in an umbrella shape. The cats climbed up the pole and slept safely above the wolves in the branches. Sometimes I would sleep up there in an old mended hammock that I hung in the tree overlooking the wolves on the floor below. Heat rises and it made a comfortable place to sleep in the winter.

I hung the third mirror vertically from the trunk of the tree house so it created a three- dimensional effect with the other mirrors and brought more light into the branches above. I then added five small mirrors to throw reflected light into the dark areas of the cave. The further the cave went back, the cooler and darker it got. I dug into the walls of the cave to make shelves for refrigeration of my dried herbs.

On one of my last hiking trips before the first serious snowfall I ventured back to the Keystone waterfalls. I didn't know it at the time, but the waterfalls are part of Keystone National Park. The wolves and I had hiked to the waterfalls often during the summer. They liked to swim in the deep pools while I sat on the bank watching. I wasn't comfortable playing in the deep water because of my lack of depth perception.

As I watched the wolves chase each other, I spied a slab of solid black obsidian stone in the water. Obsidian is volcanic glass, and has been used by native cultures to make knives and other tools. Obsidian has grounding qualities. It has the power to cut aside the layers of ego. I marveled at the perfect shape of this slab and couldn't resist taking it home with me.

While I was at the waterfall, I also filled up a bag with black sand and another bag with pure white. I figured I would use the sand for artwork during the long winter months. When I arrived home, I placed the obsidian slab over the hole in the center of my cable drum desk. It fit perfectly. Now my cave home was ready for winter.

With some natural sunlight coming in and being reflected off the mirrors, I could continue to grow a few herbs and greens in the winter. I existed mostly on dried vegetables, pancakes, vegetable stew and jerky. The few greens helped to add spice and a sense of adventure to my diet.

The biggest strain was mental and emotional. Twice a day I smoked my prayer pipe and prayed. I did beadwork and read. To stave off total boredom, I had borrowed a generator from Shane and hooked up a VCR and a small television. I couldn't watch real TV. Had there been any channels available in the mountains, the cave would have blocked the reception.

I had thought ahead and brought seven Star Trek videos, each containing four episodes. I allowed myself to watch one Star Trek episode per day until the generator ran out of gas. They helped to break up the boredom. Even though I watched the same episodes over and over, it was nice to hear someone else's voice.

Like many people confined without adult conversation, I talked out loud just to hear myself speak. It was day after day of the same old thing. You can only make so many pouches or read so many books. Besides, in the dim light, reading strained my eyes. The term vision quest seems enticing, almost romantic. The reality was a different story. In the winter, it was god-awful lonely and terribly boring.

14

Viewing Other Worlds

By midwinter, my gas generator had died. I had run out of fuel and there was no way to get down the mountain to get more. I mourned the loss of my daily fix of Star Trek. After two months, I was becoming edgy, tired of winter and tired of being cooped up in the small cave.

One day, I decided to do something different and play with the sand I had found at Keystone Falls. Sitting at my round table, I poured the sand on the obsidian slab I had salvaged from the falls. I poured black sand in one pile and white in another. I started drawing pictures in the sand like a little kid. I drew yin and yang symbols. I drew faces. Within minutes, I had sand all over the table, making incredible geometric forms.

I grabbed a star-shaped beeswax candle from the shelf and put it on the table. Not satisfied, I got up again and grabbed another beeswax candle. It was in a coffee can with a wick in the center. I lit both candles. I had never lit two candles at once, because it was too wasteful. But today I felt the need to do so.

I looked up at the mirror hanging from the cat perch. I saw my reflection, the candles and the sand painting. Then, I gazed into a mirror to my right. I could see myself in the mirror as well as my reflection in the first mirror on the left. Then I gazed into yet a third mirror. At this point I could see my reflection three times as well as the reflection of my reflection three times, for a total of six different images of myself.

Suddenly, my refection in the third mirror began to fade out and it disappeared. I had the feeling that I was seeing someone other than myself. I realized that this was not normal in any way and that I must be moving into an altered state. Another part of me reasoned that I was probably becoming extremely hypersensitive to any sound or sight because I'd been completely isolated from the world outside the cave for over two months.

Despite the weirdness of it all, I started to focus in on what looked like a man's image in the mirror. Then, as soon as I started wondering how this could all be possible, the man's image would start fading out. I would then see only myself in the mirror. It felt as if I was accessing a portal to another dimension. It felt as if I was going back in time intermittent with being in the present: alone in a cave on top of a mountain with a pack of wolves. Which was weirder? I wasn't sure. It felt as though I was moving in and out of the Akashic records.

My usual perspective on the Akashic records, when I'm doing readings, is that I look down on the records and see them as books that open into dramatic plays or film scenes that represent my client's present and past lives. In this case however, I was in the Akashic library itself, surrounded by many books. I was inside the scene from the perspective of a photograph hanging on the wall, watching the scene.

And now the scene was talking back to me! To my amazement the image of the man was writing in sand with a feather pen just as I was! His back was toward me, but I could see his face in silhouette.

"Oh my God!" I cried aloud.

He jerked as if startled and turned his head in my direction.

"Oui?" he asked.

"What is going on here?' I said, thinking I was hallucinating. "Who are you?' Where are you?' My voice raised an octave with each new question.

"Mademoiselle, parlez vous Francais?" is what it sounded like he had asked. But his speech was extremely muffled and I couldn't make any sense of it. He then turned and faced me. I don't speak a word of French but sensed that he was asking me if I spoke the language.

"Well, no." I stammered as I continued to stare at the mirror. Instead of seeing myself I saw a clearer image of this bearded French-speaking man, drawing in the sand. He looked familiar. I felt I should recognize him.

As he continued speaking in French, I searched back in my memory. There must be a reason why he looked so familiar. Suddenly, I knew. I jumped up and ran over to the bookshelf. I had about twenty books and some cassettes as well as a cassette recorder. Of course, I had forgotten the AA batteries for the tape machine so it was useless. I threw it to the side. I searched quickly through the books and found nothing. Then my eyes went to a cassette: *Conversations with Nostradamus* by Delores Cannon. It was a tape I had never had a chance to play.

"Whoa," I thought, "This is the same guy." I flipped the tape over and started reading about a sixteenth century French man who had advised the queen. "Oh my God! Are you Nostradamus?" I started blubbering.

"Yes. That is part of my name. You can speak English with me. I can understand. Who are you? What century are you? His English was hard to understand.

"I really don't know what day it is," I said. I've lost track of time. I'm living in a cave doing a vision quest. I'm living here with my wolves, my cats and a few hawks. I feel like I've been here forever so I really don't remember what year it is. My father died and I'm trying to find myself. I don't seem to be doing it very well at all." I babbled on and on, so hungry for human interaction, even under these strange circumstances. I couldn't imagine how he could understand me and I couldn't understand a word he said. I was grateful however that somehow, we could communicate. "My generator died and I can't watch TV, I whined. I'm bored and lonely. I haven't seen anyone in weeks. I'm so tired of being alone."

"What century is it?" he cut in insistently. "What year is it?" He pressed me for information, ignoring my monologue. "1989 or 1990, I don't know for sure, I said. It's cold outside and the snow is blocking the cave entrance. I haven't been outside in months. Only my wolves go outside. What year are you in?" I asked.

He told me how he served the queen and told me the year in which he was living, which I later identified as the sixteenth century. He was overwhelmingly more curious about my life than telling me about his own.

"Who is your leader?" he asked, "Who is in power?" he repeated.

I understood what he wanted to know. "We have a president who used to be an actor," I said. He's just ended his term. I'm not sure if he's a better actor or better at acting like a president," I said. "He was our 40th president. George Bush is the next president in power, the 41st president. I don't know much about him. Before that we had a peanut farmer for a president. And before that, we impeached a president. Our presidents are not born into power, we elect them."

"Such a different life, "He responded. At his urging, I told him funny stories about our presidents and our way of life. I explained the stock market, climatic change, germ warfare, and what I saw in the future. We were two people sharing our mystical views of the times, in which we were living, almost like chatting over a cup of coffee.

"Do you see me? "He wanted to know.

"Yes, of course," I said." Don't you see me?"

"No, I can only hear you," he said. Your voice is coming from my left, high up on the wall. I looked where he was pointing. There was a painting of an angel on the wall above his head." I know you are an angel," he stated, "What is your name?"

No one had ever called me an angel before and he wasn't kidding! "Well, my name is Cynthia Hart or Little Golden Bear. I am of mixed blood." Lost for words, I was afraid to tell him I had English, Welsh, German and Native blood. I was not sure he would understand.

Which name do you prefer?" he inquired. "I like both."

At the time, I didn't know who Nostradamus was. The cassette of his predictions had come to me without my having chosen it. Had I known who Nostradamus was, I would have been in total awe. Sometimes it's better not to know, I think. I was living in a cave with wolves, building a medicine wheel, and doing a vision quest. He must have thought I was strange, yet he saw me as an angel.

"I don't understand how this happened, how I connected with you, I continued. I was just sitting here drawing symbols in the sand." I explained.

"And so was I," he replied.

He asked about my cave and what I had been doing just before we had come in contact. I told him how I had arranged the mirrors to bring in as much light as possible and had noticed my image in the mirror while drawing in the sand. He asked me what a mirror was and I explained that it was an object that we used to see a reflection of ourselves in. He did not dwell on the mirrors. I had the feeling that he had quickly grasped what I had described.

"You created this connection between us by threes – you did everything in threes," he explained. You have three mirrors in the shape of a triangle. By putting two triangles together, you caused a hexagram to be formed, this is a sacred formula. Your table is a circle with a hole in the center, with a black stone on it. By using the white and black sand to make the symbols of Yin and Yang, you caused this doorway to open! It all has meaning."

I looked around the room he was in. It was nearly identical to the one I had created in my cave. We each sat at a table with a candle in the center, writing in the sand. We were mirroring each other; me in my cave, he in his room that made me think of a castle.

"Why can't you see me?" I inquired. If he understood everything that was happening, why didn't he see me like I saw him?

"Because some have the gift of seeing, some have the gift of hearing," he explained quietly. "We are different but the same."

Totally overwhelmed by everything, I tried to stand up. My legs were weak and shaking. "I think I'd better go," I said as I held onto the table for support.

"Oui, of course, my dear. I am going to write about you, about a woman who told me what was going to happen in the year 2000."

"Okay. It's been real." I said jokingly, not really knowing what else to say.

"It certainly has," I heard him say faintly as he faded from view.

Looking back on the experience later that day or night, I realized that I was living in a major portal and didn't even know it. Some mystic I was! With the snow isolating me from any real daylight, I didn't really know what time or day or month it was anymore. My feeling is that the Keystone Falls served as a generator and the crystallized walls of the cave fed off the energy. I could travel through time. Being on the highest mountain for miles, with a waterfall at the entrance to the cave, I had created a vortex of energy that had transported me. When I had set up the mirrors, it created the perfect conduit from one plane to another. If I had been a person who wasn't in tune with my inner nature at all, that long winter and that incredible experience with Nostradamus would probably just have felt like a very unreal, hallucinatory experience brought on by the isolation. As a sensitive person, however, I realized that I had, in fact, traveled through time and met one of the greatest prophets of all recorded history.

If I had known whom I had been talking to, I certainly would have asked him a lot more appropriate questions! It wasn't until a couple of years later that I started to read his work. I feasted on Nostradamus's symbolic language and his quatrain writing style. When I read in Nostradamus about the woman who shared her vision of the 20th Century, I wanted to believe he was writing about me. Perhaps he was. After all, time is quite likely an illusion.

15
Rabbit Stew

I had been cooped-up in the cave for three months straight. Day blended into night, and night into day. I smoked my prayer pipe twice a day, every sunrise and sunset. With the snow blocking the entrance, there was no natural light at all, except for what was being reflected by my mirrors. I had lost all track of time.

The gas for the generator lasted only about a month. After that, there was no more Star Trek. There were no diversions. No company at all except the animals. As the days passed, I became feverish with a true "cabin fever." Sometimes it was hard to drag myself out of bed. I was tired of reading, beading, and doing leatherwork.

My food supply was dwindling. I ate fruits, nuts, vegetables, and jerky. While I knew I wasn't getting enough protein, I ceased to care. I drank coffee, water, and herb teas. Since time had lost all meaning, I have no idea whether I ate, or not, every day. I occasionally felt hunger, but not often. I forced myself to clean the cave every day, otherwise, the animal smell would have become unbearable and my life would have seemed totally meaningless. I lived in my bed a lot of the time. I could read, make things, and I was comfortable there. My bed was dug out of the cave on a large shelf, as big or bigger than a king size bed.

I had put in a round glass window to see out of, not knowing that because of the north wind, I would have to cover it to keep the freezing air out. I had a lot of quilts and fur hides to keep me warm in bed. This was the warmer side of the cave because the wood stove heat traveled toward my bed. Before I'd realized the problem with putting a window in the north I had loved looking out over the Cascade Mountains and knowing I was living in them.

The wood stove was a 50-gallon rusted steel drum, lying on its side, with a fireplace rack holding it up. For ventilation, I had run a pipe out of the top of the cave, which was right next to the front door. I even added a little door to my stove, with hinges to open and close it. I put a damper on the pipe to control the heat flow, which took me almost a day. It worked well enough. It was one of the few things I had done correctly. I had placed a pan of water on top of the stove to steam the air. This pan also provided my hot water for bathing and hot drinks. The water came from the snow outside.

I opened my cave door one day and was confronted by a solid wall of snow. In a panic, I wondered how I was getting enough oxygen. Then I realized that the stove pipe was letting out smoke but that the melted snow around the stove pipe on the outside of the cave was letting oxygen in. For good measure and a psychological boost, I left the front door open a foot to the wall of snow. It made me feel as though oxygen could come in through the snow itself. I was also getting air through the North side window that I had covered with a hide because so much freezing air had been coming in. What had once seemed like a bad idea was now helping tremendously.

To start my furnace, I would use the formula of a small amount of newspaper, one pinecone, and two small logs. I kept it going all winter. It would often get hot in the cave. For cooking purposes, I had found an old propane stove from an RV, with four little burners and a medium sized oven. Shane and She-Bear had gifted me with six propane refills so I had plenty on hand.

Considering my primitive surroundings life was good, although extremely boring. During this time, my wolves went in and out through the tunnel they had dug near the entrance to the cave. Air came through the tunnel they had dug as well. They spent their time hunting and bringing home their prey. They brought home mice, rabbits, birds and other small animals.

One day, Bear came home with a rabbit clenched in his teeth. He came up to the bed where I was lying, tossed his head, and pushed the rabbit up against my hand.

"What am I supposed to do with that, Bear? Get it out of here!"

He stood in front of me, not budging. "No," I said firmly, "I don't want your food."

Bear pushed the rabbit against my hand again. "Take it," he said. "Get up and eat." Maybe I was just hearing voices, but I heard distinct words coming from my animals. They seemed to chatter incessantly.

"I don't want it. Leave me alone. I can't eat that." I objected.

Bear moved off a couple of feet and laid down facing me. He kept the rabbit clenched between his teeth and kept his eyes focused on me. After a lengthy standoff, I finally gave up.

"Oh, all right. You are so pushy." I glared at Bear, but my words made no impact.

I pushed myself off the bed and went over to the propane stove. With a prayer of gratitude for its sacrifice, I took the rabbit from my wolf. I grabbed my large knife and slit the rabbit in two. Without really knowing how to do it properly, and considering it an unpleasant job, I skinned and cleaned the rabbit. I put it into the pot with some herbs and dried vegetables and mushrooms and turned the heat to simmer. As it started boiling, it began to stink terribly. From time to time, I skimmed the rabbit fat off the top of the pan and dished it out into the wolves' bowls. They loved it.

I went back to bed, wrapped up in my robe and resumed reading a book on how to become a Shaman. I can tell you that to this day, I haven't found a book yet that can tell one how to become a Shaman. It seems to me it's the experience of life that transforms a person.

After an hour, of boiling the rabbit, a delicious smell filled the room. Obviously, I was very hungry. I got up and threw in some dried vegetables. I was starting to get excited about the rabbit stew. My appetite had returned.

As the smell permeated the small living space, I became ravenous. It felt like Thanksgiving.

When I could wait no longer, I took my dinner from the stove and ate it rapidly. It was so good that I totally overate, giving the bones and some meat that I was not sure of to Bear and Wolfa. Afterwards I curled up in my bed and kissed Bear for the great dinner. He always stayed at my side. We slept for hours.

I have not eaten another rabbit since that time in the cave and I have nearly become a vegetarian. It was hard cleaning that rabbit. I believe that if you eat meat, you should be willing to kill and clean it yourself. Otherwise, you are forcing the butchery karma on someone else.

In the months that we spent together, it was the wolves that taught me about survival, not my books. When I got depressed and didn't feel like taking care of myself, they took care of me. That was a big lesson because I had always been proud of myself for being independent. Over that very long winter, however, the wolves taught me a lot about interdependence, and that we all must rely on each other.

16

The Mushroom Journey

As spring started to emerge in the mountains, my wolves spent more time outside. When they returned, their fur smelled of spring. They also became rambunctious and spent a lot of time mating. I tried to shove them outside but they seemed to revel in my discomfort.

As the snow melted, I ventured out for short periods. It was still very cold, but it felt wonderful to escape the four walls. I would go out in the late evening so the light wouldn't blind me. I smelled life all around me. Deer, rabbit, and elk walked upon the awakening earth. I caught their scent even before I saw their tracks.

One day I woke up hungry and decided to make myself a salad. I got up and threw off my buffalo robe. I didn't even bother to get dressed. I had a few greens stored in my makeshift cooler. The day before, I had discovered some watercress and edible greens by the stream, down the hill from the cave. This morning, I grabbed the greens, a few dried tomatoes, onions, garlic, and reached for a jar of dried mushrooms I had put away for a treat. I stirred my dry salad around in the bowl. I was feeling sorry for myself and thought that maybe greens were the answer.

I wanted to return to civilization. My body was aching from the cold and lack of activity and light. I was lonely. My heart was heavy and there was a sadness I just couldn't shake. I had discovered that living alone was not as easy as I had once imagined. I wanted some attention, a bath in hot water, and a back rub. My stash of chocolate had been devoured long ago.

"I must be going nuts," I said out loud. "I could be home eating black licorice and bonbons instead of a dry boring salad. I'm sick of this place!" I screamed my frustration at the wolves. Of course, they ignored me. They had their minds on other things.

"Why in the hell am I doing this?" I shouted to no one. The walls were silent, mocking me. I sat on the edge of my bed, enjoying the salad. By the time I was finished eating, I had begun to sweat. Tears welled up in my eyes and spilled down my cheeks. I started hallucinating. The walls were moving as though they were breathing. The room was closing in. I started laughing at everything.

My emotions began releasing at full force. My nose and eyes were running. My head was hot and my throat felt extremely dry. The wolves looked strange. I got up from the bed and ran for the water jug. Tipping the jug, I drank nearly the entire container before stopping to breathe.
"What's going on Spirit?" I shouted. "Is this a Shaman thing or are the elders playing with me?"

I had placed a crystal in the window and it was reflecting spectrums of light all over the cave walls. There were splashes of color everywhere, with geometric patterns kaleidoscope in and out. Now my depression was replaced with wonder. I started to write and draw the things I was seeing on the dirt floor and the walls. I was seeing worlds upon worlds in the mirrors. I was talking to Spirit, God, White Wolf and anyone else I thought would listen.

The light in the cave was changing. The sun was going down. I wanted to go outside. My body temperature was getting hotter and hotter. Everything was changing from one moment to the next. "Damn it!" I screamed. "I could die here and nobody would even know what happened."

I got up and paced around the room. I screamed, "Who needs this shit?!" I was feeling sorry for myself. I was angry at the world. I was literally mad. As I paced the room, the wolves grew quiet and kept their eyes on me as I raged on.

"God, it's hot! I need to get out of her!" I ran around the room naked, pouring water on myself, trying to cool down. Circling the room, I downed massive amounts of water. I pushed past the wolves, heading for the entrance. I clawed my way through the snow like an animal. I flopped out of the cave into the snow headfirst, and then rolled over on my back, passing out.

Not really knowing how long I had been there, I came to slowly. Everything was foggy and looked strange. I tried to get up and my back hurt where it had made direct contact with the frozen snow. Since my car accident, years earlier, I no longer had full range of sensation in a lot of my body. I felt either numbness or pain and very little in between.

I edged myself up carefully. I stood upright and looked down at the impression in the snow. It was a snow angel with a big butt. The snow had melted four or five inches around the spot where I had lain.

I slowly moved back into my cave house. It was damn cold outside. When sensation started returning, I was sure I was going to die of frostbite, kidney shut down, or something. As I walked toward the bed, I passed a mirror. I stopped in my tracks despite the cold. I was still totally naked, but my body had changed. My back was beet-red, my front was a pasty white. The snow, while possibly saving my life, had toasted my skin. I stared at the mixed-blood female in the mirror and started laughing hysterically. My true nature had finally come out. My back end was red, my front end was white.

I yelled "Half-breed!" at the image in the mirror.

"That's right," the image yelled back. "It is a good day to die."

I walked over to the jars of mushrooms and realized I had eaten the wrong ones. The ones I had bartered for were still untouched. Instead I had eaten from a jar I had picked myself in the late fall. I had planned to take them to an expert I knew in town to see if they were edible. I was too afraid to eat them without an expert opinion. Now, I had accidentally used them on my dinner. I never was so sick in my life.

I used some homemade comfrey root and lemon balm ointment on my back. The pain from the snow burn was quickly setting in and I was afraid of infection. I wrapped myself in a white sheet that a favorite grandmother from Colorado had given me as I had left on my journey. Lying on my side, in my sheet and buffalo robe, I desperately wished that she were here to comfort me.

I had to go to the bathroom. My back was hurting but I still had to go. My head throbbed as I stood. I decided to go out to the outhouse. I could kill two birds with one stone. I'd be going to the bathroom and getting some fresh air. I went up the hill in rubber boots, a blue shirt, and not much else, wobbling all the way. I sat in the outhouse for what seemed like a few minutes. I was confused about where I was. I wasn't sure how to get back to the cave.

As I started heading back toward the cave, I realized that everything was white, the roof of the cave, the doorway, everything. I noticed the angle of the mountain slope seemed like it was on the wrong side. I took a few more steps and over the side I went! My foot caught on a root branch about five feet down and there I stopped. I looked around and realized I was hanging by my boot, upside down, half-naked, on the side of a cliff.

Now what do I do? I was getting dizzy and my leg hurt. I started yelling for Wolfa, but I didn't think the wolves could hear me since I was down over the edge of the embankment by about five feet. I was yelling my ass off! All I could think was, "Here I am, upside down, hanging off a cliff, and no one is going to find me. Spirit, what's up? What did I do wrong? Why me? I want to go home."

Suddenly, I heard a snarl that was not the wolves, a bear, or a human. It was the female mountain lion that was living above us at the cave with her cubs.

"Oh, no! She's going to eat me," I thought, "What can I do? Where are the wolves?"

As I was looking up at the mountain lion, she started peeing on the root that held my ankle. It was going all over me.

I was so mad I started yelling, "Get out of here!"

She started digging out the root that held me. I looked down and despite my poor eyesight I saw that the root was all that was holding me from falling about four stories. She continued digging at the root until my foot broke free from it and I dropped down onto a ledge below, right on my ass.

I was madder than hell. My ankle was by now really hurting. I tried to take off my boot but I couldn't get it off. It was just too painful. I knew it was broken.

Now what? I look up again and the mountain lion was looking down at me. Then she let out a yell that scared me half to death. Then as quickly as she had appeared, she was gone.
To my surprise, the wolves showed up suddenly. Wolfa jumped down onto the snowy ledge and licked my face. It was like she was saying, "Hey, why are you down here?" She pulled me forward and I saw that there was a small goat path that I could climb to get back up to the edge of the cliff again.

I held on to her as she pulled me onto the path and slowly but surely led me home. My twisted ankle kept me from walking upright but I found a big wide branch to use as a staff to lean on as I inched along. Bear had found part of my shirt and brought it to me. I was exhausted by the time I made it back to the cave. I sprawled out on my bed and passed out.

I woke up to a Lakota elder standing in the doorway. His rugged face reminded me of Sitting Bull or Black Elk. The elder set down. I offered him some corn bread, but he ignored my offer.

He just looked at me and said, "Are you stupid?"

I was confused. "What are you talking about?" I questioned.

"Aren't you here for a spirit journey?" He replied. "Did you think that the mountain lion was going to eat you? She was saving you. She lives above your cave. You've been taking care of her. You give her and her cubs above you the heat from your fire. Your wolves have been sharing their food with her. She followed you and helped you get free of the root. She sprayed you to mark you as hers, so no other animal would bother you. She also called for your wolves. She is your friend and yet you scream at her like that? Wake up! Stand in your true nature. You are not only human. You are spirit. The mountain lion knows that. Your wolves know that. Are you not on a vision quest?"

Feeling a little dumb, I looked up to speak. There was no one there. He was gone. I fell back on the bed and slept.

In a few days, my skin was peeling like a snake from the snow burn. I was lucky to be alive and not hurt any worse than I was. My foot was sprained. It looked like the cat had dragged me in. I had learned a lesson by overdosing on hallucinogenic mushrooms. The weird part was that I hadn't planned or intended on it. I had faced my true self by accident. Spirit had moved me.

I sat there with that red and white image of myself burned into my brain. I wish I could say that on that day I learned to accept myself and that I've never struggled with self-acceptance since. The truth is that I seem destined to repeat this lesson. Learning to love and respect myself is a constant, ongoing challenge. It's a lesson I hope to one day master.

Today when I see the mountain lion, I am not afraid. I love her. I respect her nature. She taught me to respect the life around me. I thank you, Spirit. It's a good day to be alive.

17
My Wolf- Bear Bear

Spring surrounded me as I prepared to leave my cave and rejoin society. I spent days cleaning the cave and removing all the found manmade things that I had brought inside. I removed the mirrors I had hung, swept every inch, and returned the cave to its original condition as best I could. I was feeling restless as I worked. It was hard to be inside after being cooped up all winter.

One day I finished my chores and walked outside. The wolves had long since disappeared and were nowhere in sight. I figured they were out hunting or just plain running, enjoying their freedom. I walked slowly to my garden, scouring the ground. I needed to finish the medicine wheel before I left this land. Searching for the right stone to complete the wheel, I spotted a big rock a few feet away, lying on its side. I picked it up and carried it up the hill to the medicine wheel. This rock symbolized Eagle, and the time for me to fly. I laid it carefully in the wheel to the East and stood up to survey it. The wheel was complete.

I turned and started walking back down the hill, heading to a stream where I knew watercress and other herbs were growing. I was hungry.

As I approached the stream, I heard those bubbling sounds that water makes as it travels over the rock on its relentless path down the mountain to the sea. Everything was clean and bright and fresh. Even the air smelled clean, rinsed pure by an overnight snowfall. I bent down and started to pick greens, holding them in one hand as I picked with the other.

The sound of a gunshot rang through the silence. One, and then another tore through the still air. My heart plummeted from my chest to my navel in a terrifying freefall. I couldn't breathe for a second and my chest felt tight. I didn't know what the shots meant. They horrified me enough that I started heading for the medicine wheel. From there I could see for hundreds of miles in any direction. I knew that if I heard a gunshot it would probably be a hunter shooting an animal.

I scanned the mountainside in the direction of the shots and saw the wolves, running right to me. They knew exactly where I was, even though they were miles away. I watched them as they ran up the mountain, away from the dark spot of his body, lying still and lifeless.

I ran toward them, in the direction of the medicine wheel. As I stood in its center, we all caught up with each other. They began jumping all over me. Wolfa was howling in pain, so my hands scanned her body for injuries. I found nothing wrong with her and looked around. Wolfa's six young puppies were jumping and circling, kicking up rocks with their feet. Wolfa escaped my grasp and resumed wailing.
"Wolfa, what's wrong?" I screamed as their frenzied energy infused me. Everything was distorted. It felt like time stood still. "Wolfa, what's the matter?"

"Oh god," I wailed as the realization hit me. "Bear!" I looked around frantically. "Where is Bear?" As I screamed the words, I already knew the sickening answer.

As a pack, we ran to the cave. I pulled out my gun and I loaded it. To say I was in a rage would be a gross understatement. I'm telling you I was so enraged at that moment I could've killed.

We ran down the hill to the spot where Bear lay, blood streaming from his side. I knelt and picked him up, holding all his ninety pounds close to my chest. He was already dead. I rocked him, attempting to console his soul and mine at the same time. I screamed and then sobbed as the wolves howled around me.

After a few minutes, I took his collar off and put it around my neck. I stood up with Bear in my arms and wrapped his body around my neck and on my back.

I carried him back up the mountain. My other wolves staying right by my side as I laid him gently in the medicine wheel.

Looking down at his body, I started screaming. I was so enraged I was howling like a wild animal. I knew who had killed Bear. The angle of the bullet and the tracks in the snow led right to his house.

I walked back to the cave, grabbed the keys to the truck and threw my rifle in the front seat, wishing I had my bow. The wolves leaped into the back and together we drove down to the alcoholic's house.

Spring rain and melting snow had made the dirt road impassable. Halfway down, the ground got very soft and I was soon stuck. I jumped out the drivers' window, gun in hand, and started walking toward the Neanderthal's ranch. Getting there, I looked around the yard. No one was in sight. I yelled for him.

"Come out, your ass hole!" Even though locals had told me that this same man had raped more than one woman, and I had already had the experience of him trying to corner me, I had no fear. I was going to shoot him. I didn't know what else to do. I was so angry I was out of my mind.

I pushed open the door of his house, throwing my full weight against it. With my rifle raised, I strode purposefully through the house. "You've destroyed a beloved member of my family. Now I am going to destroy some of your property!" I yelled.

Taking the blunt end of the rifle, I smashed all the windows in his kitchen and living room. When I couldn't do damage quickly enough, I raised the rifle and put holes in the walls. I walked out the door, slamming it so hard the hinges bent.
I crossed the yard quickly and threw open the door to the barn. Going from stall to stall, I released every animal from its pen, urging them on to freedom and to find their shelter elsewhere. "Go! Leave this place! Find a better life," I urged.

I wanted this man to feel pain. He had threatened me both physically and sexually. He had killed my best friend Bear. I wanted him to hurt as much as I did. He must have known I was there, because I couldn't find him anywhere.

In the midst of my agony, I realized that I was out of control. I decided I'd walk to the nearest town. I would go to the sheriff's department and turn myself in. Cold, hard facts had jarred me out of the mental state I was in. I realized that if I had succeeded in killing this man I would now be going to jail. I thought I'd better turn myself in before anything else happened.

I pushed open the door of the small sheriff's office, where two men in uniform sat behind a large desk. I was reminded again that this was a small town, as they started smirking when they saw me. They were trying hard not to laugh out loud. I must have been a sight, walking in flanked by wolves, my hair full of feathers, adorned with Indian jewelry and my feet in moccasins even though there was still snow on the ground. I was wearing this huge coat I'd made from a lama skin. I must've looked like Phyllis Diller or Big Bird. The coat was stained with Bear's blood and I was still wearing his collar around my neck. I had been in prayer prior to the gunshots and hadn't planned on a trip to town. I hadn't had a bath in weeks.

I leaned against the counter. Slowly one of the deputies walked toward me. "I just want you to know that I'm going to kill a man. The reality is this - you can either stop me or I'm going to kill him."

The deputy calmly asked, "Well, who ya gonna kill?"

"A man threatened me." I recounted the experience of the mountain lion scaring him off. I told them about my enraged retaliation. "Now he has killed my wolf. No man is going to kill a member of my family just because he can't get a piece of ass." I don't remember my exact words but I know they were very vulgar.

The deputy laughed nervously. "Oh, that's Alan. He's an alcoholic. He has raped women. He's a real jerk. We keep our eye on him as best we can. It would be best if you stayed as far away from him as possible."

"Aren't you going to arrest me?" I asked. "I want to kill him."

"No. Although if you had shot him, you would probably be doing us all a favor," the other deputy chided. They both had a good laugh again. I was in too much pain to understand what was going on. I think they figured that by the time I got back up the hill, I would've cooled off. They also said that Alan would most likely stay out of sight for a few days.

I talked with them for about another hour. I cried my heart out. I ranted and raged. They were sympathetic and understanding. I decided they knew what they were doing. They said they would talk to him, which finally quieted me. It was a good thing I was in a small town, where these officers had some leeway. I found out later that Shane had stopped in to tell them I was up there on his parents' property in the fall. They were all friends. Shane had been worried about me living up there alone. He had rightfully been worried about what Alan might do.

When I arrived home, I immediately went up to the medicine wheel. Seeing Bear on the ground, my rage flared again. I put my hands down on Bear, stroking his fur. I held his head gently in my lap.

By this time the smell of blood had brought all the animals down to the circle. The mountain lion appeared beside her loudly crying cubs. Overhead a hawk circled, screeching, while rabbits and a single opossum scurried nearby. Three elk and one mule deer also joined the circle. They pawed at the ground restlessly and snorted. I had sometimes shared food with them during the winter. Now, they shared in our grief. The wolves circled, howling a plaintive wail. Even the little domestic kitten I had found and named Snowball showed up.

With all the animals around the ridge, I started crying. I got mad at God. I ripped up the medicine wheel. I tore down all the crystals. I hated God. I hated everything.

"Bear, by God I'll do something about this," I promised. I jumped up, the gun still in my arms. "Damn, why did it have to be Bear?" I screamed and I yelled and stomped my feet. In a rage, I threw the gun down and watched it break into two pieces. I dropped to my knees. "Oh no! Not another failure! Now I can't even shoot that son of a bitch."

I started beating the ground with my both hands, my fists balled tight. I threw back my head and howled, then resumed pounding the ground. Around me the rest of the animals were howling, snarling and screeching. Even the young ones joined in.

The truth be told, as I hit that dirt over and over, my hands started transforming. White fur grew out of my hands and up my arms. Looking down my nose, I realized I had a snout. A rich, all-white fur covered my stomach and legs. I was pounding, yelling, and howling. Surrounded by all the animals, we wailed our grief together. I threw up my arms, still howling.

Above me in the shadows of dusk stood an elder I didn't know. He looked down at me gently. I looked up and jumped to my feet. I was myself again, without the wolf features. With a heavy heart, I picked up a nearby shovel and began to dig a hole. When I had finished, I pulled Bear's favorite blanket from the clothes line and wrapped him up inside it with sage, cedar and his squeaky toy. With the setting sun, Bear was buried safe in the ground.

"Little Golden Bear, it is time for you to go to Sundance," the voice of an elder said. "But first, what is the lesson this has taught you?"
I stared into his coal black eyes, staying silent for a moment. Suddenly I saw it clearly. "Oh my God!" I blurted. "I transformed and became a white wolf. Bear's soul went into me. He has become part of me." I fingered his collar around my neck. "Bear sacrificed his life. He is now walking with my spirit to protect me. The gift I have from Bear is the strength to walk with power in

teaching the feminine ways of Spirit. Bear makes sure that my female spirit is always protected."

The elder nodded and was gone. I didn't realize until that moment that most of my visits from elders were spirits. I had assumed that they were in a physical body. But no one could disappear so quickly. Exhausted, I walked back to the cave and fell into bed.

The next morning, I got up and took a walk. Before I left the land entirely and went to Sundance, I had one more mission to accomplish. I had come to the Cascade Mountains for a reason.

I had gone back to the Lakota Nation after my dad had died and tried to return his pipe to the Nation's elders. It was an important pipe, a clan pipe. They didn't want it from me, a half-blood white woman.

I was totally devastated and had asked one of the elders, "Grandfather, what should I do with this?"

He replied, "Do a vision quest, perhaps in the mountains. Spirit will show you what to do."

So now I had the prayer pipe with me everywhere I went. I carried my father's prayer pipe clenched in my hand, wrapped in buffalo hide, with sage and tobacco on the inside. I walked for a couple of miles until I knew I had found the right spot. Scraping aside the snow, I dug into the soft earth. I laid the pipe in the earth and I prayed. I covered the pipe with earth.

"Thank you, father, White Buffalo, for the gift. I have found my medicine."

I knew it was time to leave. I felt bad about destroying the medicine wheel, but later found out I had done the right thing. An abandoned first year wheel is to be dismantled.

I had found white wolf, my female medicine. I had found buffalo, my male medicine. Now I carry them inside me. I am Little Golden Bear.

As the elder had instructed, it was now time for me to Sundance. I would dance for my father, my family, and all my relations. Thank you, Spirit. Let us all walk, in peace and beauty.

18

The End of My Year

After burying the pipe, I knew I had spent my last day at the cave. After bathing and cleaning up, I packed my few belongings and prepared to leave the mountain. When you don't have much, moving doesn't take long.

I thought I'd drop off some of the gifts I'd made to She-Bear, Shane's Parents, and the postman who dropped my letters to the post office and several times brought my letters halfway up the mountain and tied them to a tree in a plastic bag for me to pick them up. When I was alone, and it was quiet, and I needed something to do, I would crochet. With each stitch, I would pray for the recipient, people that were helping me on this yearlong vision quest.

I remembered something that my Welsh grandmother once told me, "Sit down and pray, girl." It was difficult for me to pray to God. I would talk to God but, I really didn't understand what the word 'pray' meant. Church prayers, with their prescribed words, seemed too impersonal. I just liked to talk to God.

I told her I couldn't sit down because it made me nervous, I couldn't even sit still to watch TV. She smiled and gave me one of the greatest gifts of love on the planet. She gave me a ball of yarn and a crochet hook and took the time to should me how to use it. She first taught me how to make a square blanket. She taught me a few different stitches, enough to work on for months.

She said, "I pray to God as I make something for someone. They are usually for family and friends, or to sell at church. The ones that go to the church are gifts that go out to a world of people I don't know. For them, I pray for peace, love, health, and happiness.

Then she began telling me the stories of the round blanket (or shawl). In the

Welsh culture, it is given to someone in the family. It means "welcome home". Whereas the blanket is given to a wise elderly man, the shawl is given to a woman for dancing. And the round blanket is given to protect your health and your wealth, and to help you to see the difference.

Who am I to change this lovely a vision? So, I joined in with my grandmother in crocheting and continued the tradition. I was making gloves, hats, different bags, vests, and all kinds of things. I still do. I make a lot of rainbow blankets. They contain all the colors of the rainbow in them. A Rainbow Warrior is the protector of the tribe for they are the wisest and strongest. The tribal goal is to live in harmony with self and nature. The rainbow blanket is to remind us that we are loved and are one with Spirit and family. I pray with my prayer pipe to help others in their difficulties and I pray for clarity. I give gratitude for my life and all that surrounds me.

I make the rainbow blankets and other colored blankets with specific people in mind. I use the colors and patterns that I feel are the most appropriate for each person. During my vision quest in the Cascades, I had even found yarn and a crochet hook early in the year when I first moved to the mountain. When I was first exploring the mountain and around the land, I found an abandoned house. I found a bathtub that I took home and the people had also left some books behind. There was a big, intriguing trash bag in the house. Inside a tightly wrapped bag inside of a bag, inside of a bag there was a huge clean bag of yarn and crochet hooks left behind by someone who had lived there.

After belly laughing for almost a half hour at the absurdity of finding this perfect bag of yarn, I thanked my grandmother for teaching me the skill and joked with her spirit that I must have a lot of praying to do! After bringing the yarn home, I decided to make a few blankets and thank the friends who had supported me on my journey. Today there are a few hundred blankets out there. I send a blessing to them all.

Throwing my clothes in the front seat of the truck and the camping gear in the back, I stuffed the goods for barter into the back of the truck. The seven wolves were gathered all around the camping gear as I lifted it into the truck.

I patted the bed of the old Ford truck and looked at the wolves, "Come with me if you want. It's up to you." They looked at each other and looked around. Wolfa jumped in the back of the truck, clearly wanting to come along. The rest of the wolves decided to stay put. With tears in my eyes, I said my good byes and wished them peace.

The past few days had been powerful. I had lived by myself for a year and survived. I had lived on this land at no cost, without any money whatsoever. I had been surrounded by and dependent upon a pack of wolves. Another species had adopted me!

The wolves had saved my life. They taught me how to live as they do. I had learned that my true nature is to be like a wolf. I am part wolf. Wolves are extremely compassionate and loyal; that is their nature. Bear's death had taught me to shape shift, to become the power animal within me.

Although I didn't see her, I said a silent goodbye and prayer for the mountain lion and her cubs. She had left the cave the day before me in preparation for moving her cubs down to the river so that she could teach them to hunt for animals coming to drink. She had saved my life at a crucial moment when I had had the hallucinatory experience with the mushrooms. In turn, she had sheltered her cubs on top of the cave where the warm smoke and steam helped to keep them warm over the winter. We had exchanged energy and I will always be thankful for her teachings. She also taught me the value of walking in silence, just as she taught me that it is ok not to say goodbye.

It was time to leave. Coming down the mountain was always a challenge. Without brakes, I had to find ways to slow myself down. Sometimes I would have to run into a gutter or bump into a tree to come to a full stop. After another harrowing ride down the mountain, I decided that when I got to town I would get the brakes fixed. I'd had enough fun in this comedy truck.

Once in town, I traded an amiable mechanic some of my medicine bags made with wolf hair for parts and labor on my brake repair. Then I went to Shane's house to say goodbye.

The cave and the surrounding forty acres that had been my home for the last year belonged to Shane's parents. They were going to build a retirement home on the site but they hadn't had the chance to spend much time there. In fact, they didn't even know about the cave on the property until Shane and I had told them. I thanked them and told them all about their land. I had left the camp clean and in workable order so that they could use it over the summer if they wanted to.

I had torn down the medicine wheel but had left the center fire pit to remind visitors there that this land is sacred. I mentioned to Shane's parents that they could bathe in the stream and about the cooking supplies and the wood I had left there. Then I left the Cascade Mountains. I was headed for the sundance grounds.

19

My Vision from Sundance

On my way to the Sundance, I went back to Sedona to see if there was anything I needed to do. I wanted to see a few people and tie up any possible loose ends. While in the mountains, I had checked in on my family every few months through letters and by CB radio that was hooked up in the truck when I came into town.

I spent the next week readjusting to civilization. When I got home, I got out my gear and put my stuff away. I was really looking forward to a shower. I went in the bathroom and it was hard to remember how to turn the shower on. The water pressure jarred me backwards and I sprayed half the room as well as myself. I made a complete mess that day. I couldn't get used to being home again. My home contained all kinds of different smells I was no longer accustomed to. I was feeling closed in.

The first person I saw was my roommate Armand. He was happy I was back. He asked me to join him for dinner at the Hart Line restaurant. With him being a gourmet chef there, of course I said yes! It was a trendy place to eat and had some of the best food in town. A friend of his was the owner and he wanted me to experience it. As we ate in the restaurant I found it was hard to adapt to being in public again. For the first week, the food I ate went right through me. My system was in shock at eating processed foods again.

The only thing that helped was fresh water cress like the water cress that had grown in the stream on the mountain. It stabilized my body so that I could get used to eating regular food again. On the mountain, I had only eaten one big meal a day and it was nice to be able to carry over some of the healthy benefits into my life in Sedona again. For four years after my year on the mountain I ate only chicken, salmon, watercress salad, ginger and lemon as a tea in water with an occasional fruit dessert.

Wolfa was pregnant. I brought her home some dog bones from our dinner. It was soon going to be time to leave for the Sundance and Wolfa would be staying behind with Armand. She was going to have fun living with one of the top chefs in Sedona! I knew she was in good hands. She would be loved, she would eat well, and she would probably get spoiled well before the puppies came.

I met up with Grandfather Hollis at the Coffee Pot. He began teaching me more about the Sundance ceremony. I worked with him and prepared for my journey. I respected and loved him, so I was an attentive student. Back then, very few white people had ever participated in this ceremony, so everyone was somewhat skeptical and tried to talk me out of it.

I was soon on the road to Sundance, traveling with a couple of friends who wanted to attend. We arrived just before the weeklong ceremony was to begin. At first the grandmothers said that I was not prepared to dance. I was a white, blond girl with rainbow streaks in my hair. I was a skinny little banshee hippie girl that looked like she'd just blown in from the jungles of Central America. Finally, after several days, Grandmother Lynn took pity on me and could see that I had a pure heart. I told her I wanted to dance for my father and to take cancer off the planet.

Grandmother Lynn took me aside and prepared me to meet with the elders. She asked if I had ever been to a Sundance before. I told her I had never been to a Lakota Sundance but I had been to one with the Ute Nation with all men, led by Red Ute and I had accompanied my teacher, Hollis Littlecreek and my friend Gray Wolf. She asked whether I was on my moon time. I told her no and answered other questions that she asked such as whether I knew the songs, rules and rituals of Sundance.

A couple of hours later, I was taken to meet with one of the elders. Wallace Black Elk was there. He interceded for me, as I found out later, asking the

Sundance leader to allow me to participate even though women very rarely ever danced at that time.

"Have you done your vision quest?" the elder asked.

"Well, I lived by myself in the Cascade Mountains for the past year," I replied, "Under the teachings of Black Elk."

Then he asked me if I had my eagle whistle and other sacred items. And then he asked me, "Have you ever been without food and water for three days?"

I laughed. "I have been living in a cave for year. I think I've gone without enough."

He looked at me like I was totally nuts. He shook his head in disbelief but allowed me to dance. I think he looked inside my heart and trusted that I was in Spirit. The elders did not know that I was Uriah White Buffalo's daughter. I never told anyone on the reservation who my father was. I wanted to prove myself.

Sitting beside me that evening, one grandmother asked, "Do you have an eagle whistle? Do you know the songs?" She asked questions and guided me. I found out her name was Catherine and that she was of mixed blood like me. Maybe that was why she compassionately took me under her wing.

The story of the Sundance ceremony is a sacred story. The details are different and personal for each dancer. Many of the details are not to be shared outside of the ceremony and the sacred circle. I am not able to convey the total experience I had during my Sundance without dishonoring the teachers, the elders, and the Lakota traditions, but Spirit says I can speak of my visions.

On the first day of the ceremony, we did a sweat lodge. The sweat lodge purifies the dancers for the ceremony. By the second day I started really going into deep visions. I danced for hours, keeping in step with the other dancers. At one point, I danced up to the ceremonial tree, then danced back to the rest of the participants. The V shaped tree drew me to it as if I was magnetized. I danced back to it and my head snapped back against the tree. I almost felt like I was flying. I danced back and forth until the tree broke the strings tied to my flesh.

When I started having convulsions, the elders hovered nearby and pulled me back to my spot at the arbor.

Suddenly I went into a vision. I was really expecting my dad, White Buffalo Calf Woman, wolves, bears, or some cool journey to appear. If I could have scripted the vision, I would have chosen something else. In that sense, it's a good thing that Spirit was in charge, not me.

I saw this man walking toward me. I especially noticed his feet, because he had sandals on.

"Why do you hate me?" He asked as he looked at me quizzically.

Now this was one strange guy. "Excuse me! I don't even know who you are! Why would I hate you?" I looked around for my power animals. This vision was certainly not what I was expecting. The man in front of me had long dark-brown hair and beautiful deep dark eyes and dark skin. But he was not Native American.

He spoke softly, "You hate me. You hate me more than anything in this world."

"No, I don't," I denied. "I don't hate you. I don't even know who you are." I continued to stare into his peaceful eyes. I could think of no reason why he assumed I hated him. I thought he was way off base.

"I don't even know who you are," I repeated. "Who are you?"

He said quietly, "My name is Jeshua, but some know me as Jesus."

"Oh, give me a break." I replied. "I'm not into Christianity. Leave me alone. This has got to be a joke." By now I was becoming perturbed. This vision was just plain nonsense, and not at all what I expected.

He shook his head. "See, I told you. You hate me."

"There are certainly things about you that I don't like, but I wouldn't say that I hate you," I countered," It's your fan club I don't like." He continued to look at me, without saying a word.

"That was one big act you pulled on the cross," I said. "I really thought you were a trickster, a coyote. You are the biggest challenge for me to come to peace with."

Jeshua spoke back to me, "What makes you say that?" he said.

"You know, all the bull about unconditional love, and yet you put a condition on yourself to die on the cross. It was all so poorly staged." I launched into a long spiel about how I knew the truth. I emphatically declared that he was a fraud. Jeshua was on the cross being sacrificed and we're not supposed to have to sacrifice any more. And how the hell could the God of Infinite Love torture his creations forever for having the very qualities He gave them? If there was ever a market for righteous indignation, I felt I had cornered it.

Throughout my whole tirade, he simply stood quietly. I realized that I was standing with my arms outstretched, my back against the tree.

"You've got me there. This is your reality, not mine," he said.

"Oh my God! I've still got Jesus on the cross," I cried. My defenses wilted. My righteous indignation went up in a puff of smoke. I suddenly understood what he was saying. "I love you," I blurted.

I was experiencing an inner peace. And in the same moment judgment was being released, leaving my soul in peace and filling me with a deep breath of life. I could hear the true words of Jesus and his true love for humanity. He was suffering so we wouldn't have to. His love got ME off the cross. His love helped me to not judge myself for the first time in my life.

For the first time since he had died, I could hear the words that my father spoke. I knew at that moment he was there with me. I realized, I was on the cross myself, and trying to get off it.

My father's old familiar sayings started coming back. One was from Saint Augustine; "He who judges only judges something he lacks within himself." Another was, "To thine own self be true" which was one my dad would constantly hit me with. I think he was trying to show me a way to see clearly know who I was and what I really wanted.

The eyes of Jesus were upon me as he reached out and took my outstretched arms. He put his arms around me. I could hear his voice as I rested my head against his chest, "I love you, little sister. Welcome home. May peace be with you".

As I floated through the vision, I saw my body. I was still standing with my arms outstretched, my back against the tree.

When I woke up out of the dream, the elder and a grandmother were standing next to me. "What did you see?" the elder asked.

"No more sacrifice. Peace on earth." I replied.

"Yeah, you got the lesson." the elder confirmed.

As soon as the vision ended, the elders gave me watermelon and encouraged me to eat it. "Here, you need this."

I ate the watermelon quickly. It tasted fantastic! I didn't realize how hungry and thirsty I was. Three days is a long time.

I promptly threw up the watermelon as my body used the liquid refreshment to finish purging my being. After a few attempts, I could \keep the watermelon down and hydrate my flesh.

At Sundance, your sacrifice is supposed to help take something off the planet, perhaps a disease like my Dad's cancer. I was dancing for my father. I now realized the real dance was for me. I could now stop suffering. For me, the Sundance journey was very meaningful. I found out that I truly love Spirit and the service I do for Spirit is truly of my own free will.

To this day, I still don't buy into Christianity, but I do see Jesus in a better and different light. I see him as a Great Spirit. I feel like he would be a great brother to spend time with. I do believe in a Creator-God-Spirit.

One of the elders came and sat beside me. "Where is your journey taking you now? Where are you going?" Everything comes full circle. My father used to say, "Home is where you hang your hat." I was finally getting his point. No matter where I go, I am always at home.

"I'm going home," I said definitively, without offering any place name. I didn't need one. I had found my roots. I had found my vision.

Figure 13. Cynthia in Sedona, 1990s

Postscript

Since the Sundance, the clarity of the moment with Jeshua is with me always. Yet, I don't remember many details of that Sundance. I remember going there. I remember the people getting ready and getting set up. Most of us were in that expectant, uncertain space, waiting for the energy to begin. When the Sundance began, we all started merging to the unified energy of the Great Spirit. We were holding this energy of the Sun and supporting each other in this collective Oneness journey together.

I remember nodding and silently acknowledging others in their pain and concern. Yet I don't remember talking at all. I felt I had become this being of Light. The fasting was familiar to me after the experience of my one year vision quest. Nevertheless, I felt my body becoming progressively more one with Spirit. I knew the moment was coming near for me to experience my vision. Seeing Jeshua on the cross, was a shock. It shocked me out of my guilt, fear and shame of being raped as a teenager. I felt I had no support. When I was with Jeshua on the cross, the drums and singing of the Sundance went silent. Much of the ego and false prophecy took me off the cross of self judgement. That moment of unconditional love from Jeshua and from myself released me from judgement of my rapist and wrongs done to me. I was now walking over the threshold to unconditional love.

It was through the experience of the Vision Quest and finally the Sundance that I really crystalized my own vision. It is not considered good protocol to speak of Sundance experiences. The reason why I am relating a personal vision from Sundance is because I hope that it will help like-minded people who have been hurt and are seeking Spirit to help them move beyond it. I prayed to White Buffalo Calf Woman and she said that our medicines are to be shared and that it's ok to share a vision.

Since then, the vision has progressed. When my grandchildren were born, I gazed into their clear innocent eyes and saw a future full of anger, guilt, fear and crisis that did not validate common life and who they will be as people.

That scared me. I wanted to create something, an alternative way of life like the community my sisters and brothers and I created in Sedona in the 1980's. I want my grandchildren to have a future to enjoy and look forward to that allows them to experience unconditional love. I've been working many years toward putting together a school for the sacred arts and a non-kill animal sanctuary like the one we have here now in Ohio. It's my hope that youth of the future can experience spiritual learning in nature and through an Earth-supportive community. I want them to have something to ground them, to spark their capacity for unconditional love. Something for them to look forward to and a vision to strive for.

The mass protests we have seen in our country since the Dakota Access Pipeline proposed to run an oil pipeline *under* the Missouri River, tell me that people are ready to work locally. Many have contacted me and are working to sustain the environment and for our resources. In doing so, they are educating the public. Our organization stands in alliance with the people of Standing Rock and other organizations that are supporting environmental sustainability and clean water. My colleagues at our organization are involved in honoring the Earth and in creating a school for sacred traditions, music, arts and philosophy. At the sanctuary, participants are using the knowledge of their ancestors, to learn who they are as individuals, how they want to live and how to create a healthy future for future generations. Thank you to our Ambassador, who prefers not to be named, for his generous and crucial support in acquiring the Ohio farm and ranch that is now the White Bison Herd Sanctuary.

Stage two of my vision is to create a lodge for all ages, to share indigenous wisdom traditions of the world. These include peace conferences and trade shows that allow participants to share and sell their knowledge and wares. I believe that in any area of the world, people can develop their own way of creating a safe and sacred space in which to learn, to share and to live. It's part of my vision to help people realize they can do that.

To quote environmentalist philosopher Daniel Quinn, "There is no one right way..." "The people who are horrified by the idea of children learning *what* they want to learn *when* they want to learn it, have not accepted the very elementary psychological fact that people (all people, of every age) remember the things that are important to them- the things they need to know- and forget the rest."

In November of 2015 my husband Charles and I were invited to bring the herd of white and brown bison, that we caretake, to a private ranch preserve in Upper Lake, California. After a year of searching for a new home in California in 2015-16 we have finally found a place where the herd lives safe, with plenty of water, across the country in Amesville, Ohio. The generous ambassador to the White Buffalo who purchased the land supports the vision that is incorporated into the mission statement of our non-profit, Sacred World Peace Church & Alliance in 2008. Together we want to create a place for arts, education and healing.

As we move into this next chapter in life, I continue my mission to create a place where people can heal and create greater personal meaning. My goal is to leave behind a non-kill sanctuary where the White Buffalo can have their space to be free, to grow and multiply. Since 2014 we began using the dba name White Bison Association with the specific mission of caring for the White Buffalo Herd and educating people about them. I'm now writing a second book about my journey in coming to know the White Buffalo Herd and becoming their caretaker.

Along the way, there are hundreds of people who have come together to help the White Buffalo survive and thrive. The core group of supporters, however, is quite small. I've learned that it only takes one person to create change. It takes one person creating something good, to have a ripple effect that can create change on a larger scale. What has been so spectacular in my life is that the Creator sends people to arrive at exactly the right time and space. They intuitively know how to help without my asking them. They tune-in to what needs to be done at the time and how they can contribute. Some will stay for longer and others contribute just a brief inspiration. It depends upon their own personal mission.

I was born blind. But I wasn't born into darkness; I was born into light. It was Spirit who turned the lights down temporarily. Then at the age of six, Spirit turned me around and I could see again. Over the years I've learned that there are many ways of seeing. I love God, only I don't call it God. I call this energy "Creator." That's what my God is – creative Spirit. It's not about being a man or a woman. It's about being part of an incredible and superior energy. We are all a part of it. Being part of the Creator is our spiritual inheritance. It's about paying attention and realizing that synchronicity is everywhere and that life is a Great Mystery.

When I close my eyes, I'm in the light of the Creator. I don't see darkness. I see light. Anytime I want to know the truth about something, I pray to the Creator. That line of connection is where my vision and my faith comes from.

My focus is on being true to myself. I don't judge other people's truths. They need to live their own beliefs and I will respect those. Our paths may cross for a long time or for only a moment. My journey is about surrendering to Spirit and finding out how I can be of service. My needs are always taken care of because I have faith. My joy, is to see All succeed in life. Through my year of vision quest, I learned that, above all, I must be true to my own nature. My few words of advice to seekers are, that no matter where your path carries you in life, stay true to your nature! Keep peace in your heart and you will always be on the path. The heart is Spirit and following Spirit will bring you home. Blessings!

Made in the USA
Lexington, KY
29 April 2019